TAKING
OVER

In Praise of *Taking Over*

"Coming from a family-owned business myself, I've learned that with the rewards come the challenges. *Taking Over* provides the necessary tools to overcome those obstacles, as well as great advice on how to grow a successful business while maintaining its core values and traditions."
—**Donny Deutsch**, Chairman, Deutsch Inc.; TV commentator; and author of *Often Wrong, Never in Doubt*

"Family business issues are as old as the Bible. Mitchell Kaneff approaches the subject in a clear, innovative way and sets the stage for future success."
—**Marcy Syms**, CEO, Syms Corporation

"Mitchell's book details the opportunities and challenges involved in leading a family-controlled business. Even better, it provides terrific tools and insights to be successful."
—**William Lauder**, President and CEO, Estée Lauder Companies

"Mitchell Kaneff's advice to family business owners is clear and concise. What's more, he provides a down-to-earth, methodical approach to the complicated and often emotionally harrowing process of passing on a family business to subsequent generations. Kaneff's vast personal experience and anecdotal writing style make this book a fun, informative read."
—**Stephen Milstein**, former CEO, Burlington Coat Factory

"This is an excellent book with great take-home value."
—**Mitchell Modell**, CEO, Modell's Sporting Goods

"Because it is grounded in his experience and passion for his business, Mitchell's book is a useful tool for those immersed in family businesses and for those who advise them."
—**Paul Sessions**, Director, Center for Family Business at the University of New Haven

"Mitchell's book presents an inside view of the special aspects of family-run companies. This is an indispensable guide for those about to embark on working in a family business."
—**Ann S. Lieff**, CEO, The Lieff Company

"*Taking Over* offers its readers valuable and practical information and insight on running a family business in today's world. If you're part of a multigenerational company, you'll benefit from reading this book."
—**Maximilian Riedel**, CEO, Riedel Crystal of America

"I wish this book had been written ten years ago. It would have been extremely helpful for my family and me. It is essential reading for every family business member, the earlier the better."
—**Ronaldo Stern**, CEO, H. Stern Jewelry

"Mitchell addresses head-on the inevitable succession issues found in every family business. Whether you're coming into or phasing out of your family's business, *Taking Over* is a must-read book."
—**Jim Warner**, author of *Facing Pain — Embracing Love*

"Every small business owner in America should own a copy of Mitch Kaneff's *Taking Over*. If you manage a small business and want to succeed, you can't afford to go another day without reading this book."
—**Granville Toogood**, top executive coach and author of *The Articulate Executive: Learn to Look, Act, and Sound Like a Leader*

TAKING OVER

OVER

Insider Tips from a

Third-Generation CEO

MITCHELL KANEFF

TEN EAGLES PRESS
New York City

Published by
Ten Eagles Press
57 West 57th Street
New York, NY 10019
www.TenEaglesPress.com

Editorial: Sandra Jonas
Cover Design: Ken Silvia
Book Design: Kayla Morelli

Printed in Canada. Cover provided by Arkay Packaging.

Publisher's Cataloging-in-Publication Data

Kaneff, Mitchell
  Taking over : insider tips from a third-generation CEO / Mitchell Kaneff.
  New York, NY : Ten Eagles Press, c2011.
  p. : ill. ; cm.

ISBN: 9780982845462

1. Family-owned business enterprises - Succession.

HD62.25 .K36 2011   658.045—dc22

2010932819

To my grandfather

MAX KANEFF

for his dream and determination

and

To my father

HOWARD KANEFF

for his love and mentorship

CONTENTS

PREFACE

In 1922, my grandfather, Max Kaneff—an orphan from Ukraine—started what was to become our family business, Arkay Printing, on the Lower East Side of Manhattan. He had already practiced his printing trade in Germany, China, Japan, and Canada, but when he arrived in the United States, he was convinced that his hard work could bring him fortune. Through the good times of the '20s, the lows of the Depression, a world war, and countless recessions, Max Kaneff struggled—and succeeded—in growing his craft into the flourishing and reputable business he'd envisioned.

In 1949, convinced that printing was the future, my grandfather sent his son (my father, Howard Kaneff) to Rochester Institute of Technology, where he could specialize in printing. This was the beginning of the second generation at Arkay.

Howard Kaneff joined the company after graduation and was tutored in the various aspects of running a business. His father placed him in sales, a role my dad practiced—and perfected—until Max's death in 1962. Max Kaneff left 25 percent of the business to his son and 25 percent to his daughter. However, Howard's mother, my grandmother, retained the 50 percent balance of the shares, thereby setting the stage for family battles.

My father later swore, after buying up the family shares over the next twenty years, that he'd never put his son in the same situation. This time, his son would be equipped to take over.

Throughout those two decades, my father periodically gifted me his stock, consequently not only settling the issue of estate taxes but paving the way to pass the baton again—to a third generation.

Of course, I would not have written this book—nor would you be reading it—had conflict not followed.

The seeming inevitability of those conflicts, coupled with the realization that there were coping mechanisms to avoid them, formed the basis of this book. I hope the stories, advice, and tools I present can lead you past the pitfalls and into the rewards of transitioning within your own family business.

ACKNOWLEDGMENTS

This book would not have been possible if it hadn't been for Richard Peirce, the headmaster of the Forman School in Litchfield, Connecticut. He encouraged me to pursue journaling as a form of expression and creativity, paving the way for twenty years of habitual writing. This practice allowed me to document—as formally as possible—the events that took place during the succession at Arkay Packaging.

I am indebted to the mentors in my life who counseled my journey and inspired me to take on the challenge of leadership and CEO. A special thanks to John Compton (RIT), Bob Glendon (TRG), and Jack Gaziano (State Street Bank). Peter Kash and Dan Nissanoff, in particular, were instrumental in motivating me to write *Taking Over*. I am also grateful to Steve Krein and Noah Katz, who recommended Strategic Coach, and to the late Dan Taylor, my coach, whose guidance played a key role in the development of this book.

I give thanks to Tom Pitner, Jim Warner, and Glenn Gordon for their spiritual direction and emotional intelligence, and to my YPO Forum mates for their confidence in me and their generous support and advice.

I want to express my full appreciation to my customers for their loyalty. I'm especially beholden to Leonard and Evelyn Lauder for modeling superb leadership qualities and compassion for their associates.

For their commitment to excellence, I owe much gratitude to all the employees—past and present—at Arkay Packaging. I particularly want to acknowledge Walter Shiels for his unwavering loyalty, strength, and teamwork, and Brian Hopkins for his perseverance, persistence, and unparalleled ability to get things done. I also give much credit to Darlene Triglia for her honesty, conviction, integrity, and uncensored opinions.

I'd like to extend my appreciation to Gregg Goldman for his stimulating and challenging insights, as well as to Kim Crawford, Kamini Advani, Kris Koertge, Frank Clark, John Sheridan, and Joan Kepco for their impressive contributions. Special kudos to Craig Bradley for his willingness to do whatever it takes to make us a better company, and to Eric Simon for his vision of the golden opportunity right in front of our eyes in Virginia—and for making it happen.

I want to thank a number of the people who assisted me in compiling this book: Scott Levy, whose friendship and open-minded sharing of management tools helped me—and Arkay—reach new levels excellence; and Jon Kaufman, wise beyond his years, who blessed me with his friendship and tough love. William Lauder, Mitch Modell, Steve Milstein, Bart Krupnick, Brian Enverso, Andrew Sussman, Michael Zimmerman, Tony Meyer, Steven Riecker, and Gary Hager shared their stories and invaluable ideas, greatly enriching my writing.

To Michael Koffler, I give thanks for his humor in my time of need and for his ability to help me compartmentalize the issues at hand, and I am immeasurably grateful to the Wallachs (Allison, Lou, Charlie, and Annie)—my extended family—who were with me when I began writing this book on the beaches of Aruba. I also offer my appreciation to Leon Bibi, the consummate warrior and musical mate, who gave me strength during exceptionally challenging times, and to my cousin Sharon Pollack, who furnished the archived photographs that appear in this book. At a glance, they provide profound insights into the history and valuable continuity of multigenerational family-owned businesses.

I thank John McCarty for organizing my thoughts, and I am extremely grateful to Sandra Jonas and Adam Reingold for editing my words and bringing them to life, charting a course of action other families can use to successfully pass their businesses to the next generation. I am indebted to Ken Silvia for his shared passion for this project and his amazing creative direction, and to Ruth Rugoff for her calm, professional approach and assistance with this book's assembly.

I have saved my deepest appreciation for those closest to me.

To my in-laws, Edie and Arthur Kronenberg, I want to express my gratitude for believing in me and making me feel like their own son. And I thank my sister, Viviane, for cheering me along my journey and never doubting me.

My father, Howard Kaneff—to whom I credit my high regard for discipline and determination—persevered through the baton-passing experience. Without his respect and optimism, the process may have collapsed. To my mom, Cherry Kaneff, who introduced me to—and helped me appreciate—the aesthetics of art and design, I am indebted for inspiring me toward perfection.

To my sons, Max and Josh, I am grateful for grounding me and making me understand what is most important. Every day they teach me patience, helping me maintain the gift of balance that I talk about in this book.

Lastly, to my beautiful bride, I give thanks for her never-ending encouragement to follow my passions and for her unflagging support, whether I am stumbling or succeeding. I love you, Amy.

If You Don't Run the Business, It'll Run You

Nick, the second-generation CEO of a commercial printing company with several factories, came into the business when his dad, Harry, suffered a brain aneurysm.

"You're going to be my partner from now on," Harry told his son from his hospital bed, though they had no succession plan or anything written down to stipulate such an arrangement.

As soon as Nick stepped in to help, he discovered no long-range business plan (or even a short-range one, for that matter) and no organizational structure, not even a human resources department. His father had purchased the company only to milk it for as long as possible until it had grown large enough for him to sell off.

Immediately, Nick set to work building an organizational structure, putting tools in place to measure sales and productivity, and initiating procedures to improve worker skills and minimize accidents. When Harry recovered and returned to work, father and son immediately banged heads over their respective visions. Harry wanted to continue siphoning off dollars, whereas Nick wanted to reinvest them for improvements.

Very quickly, the partnership Harry had dangled before his son from his hospital bed turned out to have no meaning at all. He undercut the younger man's authority and resumed his former style of management—a style that fueled fear in his employees about the future of the business and their job security. A climate of mistrust permeated the organization.

Unwilling to tolerate such dysfunction, Nick left to run an event management company at considerably more pay and considerably less stress. But then his dad got sick again and this time offered Nick a controlling 70 percent interest in the business. Nick accepted, believing his father a man of his word. He gave up his event management job and returned to work as CEO of the printing company, only to find it saddled with higher overhead, thinner margins, and deeper debt than when he had left. Once again, his dad had scammed him into taking over their beleaguered company. Harry could selfishly continue drawing cash from it (in this case, a $70,000 monthly paycheck from the sale to his son) while Nick struggled to make the business fiscally sound, raise morale, and keep his investment from going down the drain.

The Odds Are Against You

It may come as no surprise to you to learn that Nick and his dad haven't spoken in years, their relationship perhaps irreparably damaged by these unfortunate circumstances. On the other hand, it may indeed come as a surprise to learn that, apart from its details, this story is not that uncommon when family-owned businesses transition from one generation to the next.

In the United States, 80 to 90 percent of all business enterprises, or approximately 11.5 million, are family owned.[1] These organizations currently account for 60 percent of all wages paid

---

1. Melissa Carey Shanker and Joseph H. Astrachan, "Myths and Realities: Family Businesses' Contribution to the U.S. Economy," *Family Business Review* 9, no. 2 (Summer 1996): 113; U.S. Census Bureau, Statistics of U.S. Businesses, 2006.

and 78 percent of new jobs.[2] Yet here are some sobering statistics: Despite their impressive contribution to the U.S. economy, only 40 percent of family businesses will survive to the second generation of ownership, 12 percent to the third, and just 3 percent to the fourth.[3] These statistics are not unique to this country, either. In the United Kingdom, Australia, and Asia, the survival rates are just as bleak.

Why do so many family-held companies fail to survive the transition from one generation to the next? I've come up with three reasons.

First, the most senior executives or business owners don't plan for the succession process because they just don't want to face the prospect of surrendering control.

Second, no recognized successor exists to fill the role of senior executive or company leader in the event of that person's sudden death or illness.

Third, and related to the previous two, retirement has an enormous psychological impact on a large percentage of business owners and senior executives, who say they don't ever want to retire. In the 2002 Mass Mutual Financial Group/Raymond Institute survey of senior executives, 16 percent admitted they were not planning to retire, and an even greater percentage said they wanted to remain "involved in the business" even in retirement. This attitude will inevitably create tension and conflict between the appointed successor and the retired owner or senior executive, and can often lead to shattered family relationships, as Nick's story illustrates.

---

2. Stacey Perman, "Taking the Pulse of Family Business," *BusinessWeek*, February 13, 2006, http://www.businessweek.com/smallbiz/content/feb2006/sb2006021 0_476491.htm.

3. Joan Axelrod-Contrada, "More Daughters Take Lead Role in Family Businesses," *Boston Globe*, May 4, 2003.

The Third Man

When I was fifteen years old, I started working for our family business, Arkay, a leader in the design and manufacturing of value-added folding cartons for the cosmetics and health and beauty industries. At that time, we were in our sixtieth successful year of business, a feat in itself. Our list of customers included Avon, Estée Lauder, Sanofi, Charles of Ritz, and Chanel.

My father wisely suggested that if I were to take over some day, I should learn the ins and outs of the business from the bottom up. So beginning in high school, I worked summers at Arkay. For my first job, I was a packer at the end of the glue line, where the folding cartons make their last trip in the production cycle before being shipped. My shift lasted from 7 a.m. to 3 p.m., and I commuted from my folks' home in Manhattan to the plant in Hauppauge, a forty-five-mile drive.

Each summer I learned a different discipline, from loading presses with stock and mixing inks to die making and stamping hot foil leaf. I gained firsthand knowledge of the responsibilities and challenges at every level. Some of the men I worked for as a teenager are still with our company today.

I'd always had a good relationship with my dad, Howard, the second-generation owner of Arkay. He had inherited it from his own father, Max, a Russian immigrant, so my father always dreamed of eventually bringing me into the business as well. I'd met many people who had not wanted to go into their family's business for one reason or another and preferred instead to pursue careers of their own, but I was not one of them. I had always viewed going into Arkay Packaging as a wonderful opportunity, a true gift. The

The chance to take years of business tradition and history to the next level in a new millenium had always inspired me.

chance to take years of business tradition and history to the next level in a new millennium had always inspired me.

To prepare for that opportunity, I went to Rochester Institute of Technology, one of the best printing schools in the world and my dad's alma mater. There, I earned a B.S. in printing management and sciences. I wanted to obtain the fundamentals for success in my career so that if I didn't take to the family business, I could always do something similar elsewhere.

After graduation, I moved back home to Manhattan. Twenty-three years old and single, I had a ball living in the Big Apple. Before long, I received two job offers, one from an equipment manufacturer in Germany and the other from one of Arkay's friendly competitors.

Then, late one night, after partying on the town with some friends, I went into the kitchen for my customary glass of water. There, sitting alone at the table and looking quite haggard, was my father. He had always appeared to me to be a pillar of confidence and optimism. I had never seen him looking so worried. It was 1990 and Arkay had just invested millions in capital equipment to boost our leadership position in the marketplace. The company was highly leveraged, putting enormous stress on the balance sheet. The recession was taking hold, and sales were down 25 percent over the previous year. The idea of just leaving Dad alone with the business under these conditions and getting on a plane to Germany with a "good luck" wave did not resonate well with me. Instead, I asked, "What can I do to help?"

That moment marked the beginning of my odyssey toward ultimately taking on sole-shareholder responsibility for Arkay Packaging as its third-generation CEO in 1997. And when I finally took that big step, I had no carefully spelled-out succession plan to follow. Like many people in the same situation, I learned by doing and just forging ahead, resorting to trial and error most of the time.

I wished I'd had a guide for successor CEOs, and searched for one in vain. The bookstores didn't carry anything that could ease my way through the process. I found nothing to help me understand and deal with the many emotional and professional challenges I was facing. It was probably then that the idea began percolating in my mind of writing my own book—of sharing my own experiences—to help future second-, third-, and fourth-generation owner-CEOs.

I've always enjoyed writing. A former headmaster had urged me to keep journals for recording everything from my traveling experiences to daily events and inspirations. I continued that practice even when I stepped in to run the family business, tracking all the ups and downs I was going through, describing what worked, what didn't, and why. Putting everything down on paper was therapeutic for me, especially during the toughest moments.

Those notes form the basis of this book. Within these pages, you will find the help you need to ride out the storms that come with inheriting or buying into a family business—and you will learn how to plan ahead to ensure the smoothest, most rewarding transition possible for your own successor.

How to Use This Book

I've divided *Taking Over* into two parts. Where you are in the transition process determines where you should begin reading.

Part 1 focuses on the most significant emotional and professional issues you will face when first assuming control of a family business. I share my experiences and conclusions to help you develop a plan for handling the stress and challenges unique to family-owned companies. You will discover what worked for me and what didn't, and the guidelines you need to follow to achieve a successful transition.

In the first section, I also review the essential measurement tools required to run any complex business, highlighting the need for consistency to achieve a constantly growing operation. Even if you are not taking over a manufacturing operation like mine, you will need to know the key pressure points and vital signs common to all businesses—and review them daily, weekly, monthly, or yearly.

You will learn the value of building your own management team to help you deal with adversity and foster a climate of trust—as well as the ways consultants can assist you in keeping your plans from imploding or being sabotaged.

Most importantly, the first section will show you how to balance work and life. Health is wealth. Without a proper balance, the pressures of dealing with the day-to-day challenges, emotions, and egos of running a family business can wear you down.

Once you have gone through the transition and applied the material in part 1 to your experience, keep reading. The second part of the book is designed to help you plan for the next stage in your evolution as a leader. Organizations that prepare for the future have a better chance of survival than those that don't. Some might make it through the decades of pain that a lack of planning will manifest, but the outlook is bleak.

You will find out how to make passing the torch to your own successor proceed the way you want—without derailing everything the business has achieved. If you are at that stage now, skip directly to part 2. It lays out the critical steps for developing an effective succession plan, one that addresses the important concerns and interests of family members and your team. With the proper preparation, you can save your own successor from the same difficult adjustment period you may have suffered through.

Obviously, the most crucial aspect of succession planning is choosing the right successor. In my case, my sister, Viviane, and I were the only possibilities. Viviane seldom seemed interested in the business, whereas I had always been keenly so. Because most families have multiple siblings, you need to acknowledge the most competent one who is also interested in the business—and then hand over control to that person without trying to hold on to it. I will explain how to do this without feeling as if you're just rolling the dice.

One key to protecting your family legacy is assembling an estate-planning dream team, and I will show you how. Experts in different areas of estate and succession planning can counsel you on the important issues, from taxes, trusts, and wills to complex legal and financial timelines. This section will tell you how to find the right advisors and how to use them properly.

Whether you are just coming into a business or have reached the point when you're thinking about passing the baton, you will find many useful ideas, insights, and techniques in this book. The insider tips included in every chapter—thirty-six in all—will help you remember the most salient advice. You can sleep better at night knowing you have the resources at your disposal to tackle the difficulties that come your way.

Always remember this: yes, you have a responsibility to profitability, but the transition process should also be rewarding and educational, and bring families closer together, not tear them apart.

So good luck on your succession journey and enjoy every moment of it!

By 2050, virtually all closely held and family-owned businesses will lose their primary owner to death or retirement. Approximately $10.4 trillion of net worth will be transferred by the year 2040, with $4.8 trillion in the next 20 years.

—**Robert Avery,** *Initiatives*

COMING INTO THE BUSINESS

PART 1

Far better is it to dare mighty things, to win glorious triumphs, even though checkered by failure, than to rank with those poor spirits who neither enjoy much nor suffer much because they live in a gray twilight that knows not victory nor defeat.

—**Theodore Roosevelt**

ONE

Is the Job for You?
Doing Your Homework

When I came on board to run Arkay, I already knew how some of the company ticked from having worked there in various capacities almost every summer since I was a teenager. A grooming process rather than part of a succession plan, this experience helped spur my interest in—and passion for—the business. It also stimulated discussion early on of my eventually becoming CEO. (You can never talk too soon about succession in a family business, though most people often wait too long—more on that in part 2.)

But in terms of actually taking over for my dad and confronting the challenges inherent in a family business, I was ill prepared. I had to find my way mostly through trial and error on the job. This does not make for the smoothest, most stress-free succession.

With the benefit of hindsight, I developed several guidelines for CEOs or business owners to follow *before* they inherit or buy into a family-held business. By doing this work ahead of time, they can clarify their new role and help ease the adjustment period for everyone involved.

Let's explore each one in detail.

Know Why You're Here

No, I am not being New Age or touchy-feely. To prepare for the leadership position, you need to do some soul-searching and find out *why* you've gotten yourself involved in the business. Otherwise, the unavoidable challenges of taking over *any* business (let alone a family-held one) may prove twice as daunting. And you and the company could fail.

Soul-searching can be tough. You will need to confront your own ego and look at your strengths and weaknesses. You will have to ask yourself why you want to be part of the organization and what you're willing to do to succeed. Critical for accepting any position, this introspection is even more critical if—as I did—you enter the family business as heir apparent *before* the current president has begun seriously thinking about retiring and passing the baton. Always remember that you will be joining an established organization with traditions and a vision already in place.

Begin by asking yourself what you love: is it selling, crunching numbers, strategizing, working with people, or marketing? Your answers will help expose your strengths (what you have the most fun doing) and your weaknesses (the tasks and responsibilities that make you go "ugh!"). This information will guide you in assessing the type of team you will be inheriting and the type you want to surround yourself with (the two do not always mesh), and what spots may need to be changed or filled.

Knowing what you love will give you a sense of purpose, one that will motivate you to jump out of bed every morning fired up about the day ahead and eager to bring about the future you seek. This self-awareness will also help you determine whether you and the family business actually make a good match. If you have doubts, don't fool yourself into thinking that just because you're the heir apparent, the job will be easier than going elsewhere or starting something from scratch. With such a mind-set, you will surely wind up knee-deep in the quicksand of managerial headaches, family dramas, employee squabbles, and other forms of dysfunction.

Insider Tip #1

Decide if the family business really excites you. Feeling passionate about taking over the organization and genuinely wanting to shape its future are key not only to achieving a smooth transition but also to making a positive, lasting impact.

Find Out Where You're Going

On old adage says that if you don't know where you're going, the likelihood is you'll never get there—or you'll end up somewhere else. Especially when assuming the leadership of a company, you need to know where you're going. To determine your direction, begin by meeting with the majority shareholder, CEO, or board chair and finding out where the business is *now*. This can give you insights into where you might wish to take it—and perhaps even help you rough out a timeline for getting there.

Well-defined objectives are important for the new leader of any company, but they are absolutely essential in a family-held one, where the family credo very often is "This is the way we've always done it, so why should we change now?" and the current CEO is very much set in his or her ways. If you don't have a firm destination in mind, the

> If you don't have a firm destination in mind, the likely power struggle between you and your predecessor could go on for years, leading the company into bankruptcy.

likely power struggle between you and your predecessor could go on for years, leading the company into bankruptcy.

The reality is that some family members will *never* be open to you or want to listen to what you have to say. Knowing where you're going (and what you're getting into) prepares you for such difficulties, enabling you to understand them and head them off sooner. That way, you can apply your goals for the business to other, more productive areas where you won't be constantly running into a brick wall.

Insider Tip #2

Get clear about your goals to quickly gain the respect of the entire organization for addressing the company's future. Most important, you'll feel good about yourself for starting to move toward that future by developing a vision of it.

Analyze Family Dynamics

I can't help but smile whenever I hear someone running a family business, or about to inherit one, say he hasn't had—nor does he expect to have—any difficulties with the family. I smile because I know that this is rarely the case. Confronting relatives is one of the hardest parts of the leadership job in every transition.

The parent-child relationship is always a challenge, even without business matters getting in the way. I am blessed with a truly kind, generous, and mentoring father, but as you will see later, we had our own share of trouble when I started running the business. The respect we've always had for each other helped us move past our differences, though not every successor to a business is as fortunate.

Besides the parent-child relationship, brothers, sisters, aunts, uncles, and the other parent can enter the mix. I know of one company owned by three brothers, two of whom got together to kick out the third because they had their own sons working there and didn't want the exiled brother's younger offspring working there as well. Also, I've heard of family members—aunts and uncles—who are on the payroll in a nonworking capacity but make decisions at board meetings that affect (often negatively) the company's operations. When money and power are added to family dynamics, every exchange can lead to conflict, and quite frequently an explosion occurs, destroying both the business and the family.

> When money and power are added to family dynamics, every exchange can lead to conflict, and quite frequently an explosion occurs, destroying both the business and the family.

Even in the best of situations, you won't be able to completely avoid family problems. The sooner you accept this, the sooner you can uncover and address potential pitfalls. Take these steps early on to minimize the fallout:

1. Find out which family members are actively working in the business and who among them owns stock.

2. Determine if any nonworking family members are stockholders.

3. Evaluate the working stockholders' job performance and weed out incompetence.

This last step is absolutely necessary. Aunt Sally and Uncle Harry may own stock, but that doesn't entitle them to their jobs if they fail to perform up to snuff. Buying out and replacing unqualified family employees can be incredibly difficult. Be prepared to confront this brutal fact head on. If you feel you can't stay objective or the situation is too delicate, hire an outside consultant to assist you in propelling the process along.

Insider Tip #3

Examine family values and emotional issues as they relate to the business *before* you take over. Trying to do this later, when you're on the job, is like trying to get the lay of the land from a foxhole.

Seek Outside Guidance

Unless you are a magician, you might (and probably will) need some support when dealing with family members (not to mention employees, customers, and vendors) of various ages and generations. From the Greatest Generation to the baby boomers to Generation X and beyond, each group has its unique worldview and approach to doing things.

An industrial psychologist can help bridge those generational gaps. One part strategist and one part Dr. Phil, this type of business consultant can effectively referee one-on-one meetings or even facilitate group meetings between you and other family members or constituencies. That way, you can keep the momentum driving forward rather than becoming logjammed.

After I took over the business, my father and I hired an industrial psychologist to help us resolve some communication and management-style difficulties. The psychologist showed us how to improve our listening skills so we could really hear what the other was saying—and gave us the tools to more openly express what we wanted and needed from each other. These refereed meetings provided an ideal venue for venting our frustrations, concerns, desires, and goals, and for sharing our vision of our current and future roles in the business.

An outside advisor can help you handle conversations in a more objective way without a lot of emotional interplay. Stand-offs can be avoided or brought to an end. Dates can be arbitrated and set for milestone changes as the baton is passed on. And plans can be more smoothly orchestrated. Chapter 4 delves into how to best utilize consultants when you assume control of a family business.

To find an industrial psychologist, search the Internet for "family business centers" and select one in your area from the list of resources. See appendix B for other recommendations.

Insider Tip #4

Don't hesitate to turn to consultants for help. Not only can they shave years off the transition process, but by reducing stress, they can *add* years to your life as well.

Accept Fiduciary Responsibility

One of my favorite business books is *The Goal: A Process of Ongoing Improvement* (3rd ed., North River Press, 2004) by Eliyahu M. Goldratt and Jeff Cox. It tells the story of a manager, Alex Rogo, who has three months to turn around his failing production plant in order to save his livelihood and that of hundreds of other people.

To accomplish that goal, he asks himself why they're in business: is it to help meet customer needs, keep people employed, take care of our families, or bolster the local economy?

And the answer he comes up with is this: to make money! Why is that the answer? Because without generating revenue, a business can't do anything else: it can't invest in new technology to grow the business, hire or advance employees, support customers with innovation, put food on the table, add value to the community—*nada*. Being fiscally responsible is the number one rule of all. Without that, all bets are off.

In a family business, some people on the board, either payroll workers or stockholders, may feel entitled to and demand high compensation simply because they belong to the family. They don't care if they might jeopardize the company's future. All businesses have cycles, and yet relatives often feel they deserve wages out of line with the current realities of smart fiscal policy. *They want what they want, and they want it now.* So before you assume leadership, make sure you look at the amount going out to each family member and determine if it matches the industry average for a particular position or role.

> In a family business, some people on the board, either stockholders or paid employees, may feel entitled to and demand high compensation simply because they belong to the family.

Set up a yearly profit plan with a budget—and a strategy for enforcing it—that promotes financial accountability. Keep this in mind: anything that can be measured can be managed and improved.

Insider Tip #5

Hit the ground running by reviewing your relatives' salaries prior to taking the helm. Establish fair compensation for each position based on performance and market standards, not on a family member's demands.

Love It or Get Out

This guideline goes hand in hand with knowing why you're here. Having a great passion to shepherd your new business will lead to an unwavering determination to do the best job possible and to take the company where you want it to go, no matter what. In my case, passion fueled my will to win, keeping me motivated. Whenever the business suffered setbacks or I ran into any obstacles that threatened my plans, I refused to back down.

In my early days as leader of Arkay, I overheard my father on the phone with one of our customers. Before I could intervene, the conversation had overheated to the point that we lost a major customer's business. With single-minded perseverance, I finally healed this relationship, but it took over six years.

You are (or will become) the face of the company to your employees, customers, and vendors, so you want them to see your passion and your commitment to them and the business. If they don't, they'll start placing bets on how long you'll stay in your job or how long the business will last. Most of them will have seen this movie before in their work lives and will already know the ending. If you don't believe in what you're doing, they won't either, and you might as well get out now.

The business was not created by you, but by some other relative from a previous generation. You've got a legacy to live up to that isn't yours. Sometimes those shoes can be very hard to fill.

Insider Tip #6

Be honest with yourself. If you don't share your predecessor's passion, do him, yourself, and everyone else a favor and relinquish the role to another successor or buyer. Go all the way—or go home.

Have an Exit Strategy

All businesses struggle with change. But changes in the temperature of the marketplace are one thing. They're expected, and everyone within the organization usually knows how to weather them. A change in management is another thing altogether. When no succession plan exists, the unforeseen death of the principal man or woman just throws everyone and everything into chaos. Because my father didn't want to wreak such havoc on our employees or jeopardize Arkay's future in any way, he consciously started early on to build a system for replacing him.

Who will be taking over? Will he be capable? Will the business survive? Will I have a job? Without a plan in place, questions like these can ripple throughout an organization, turning morale, productivity, and ultimately profits upside down. But when change in leadership is fully anticipated and carefully thought out, everyone breathes more easily and remains calm. They feel more confident about the business's future and therefore about their own future as well.

When you accept the reins of a family business, then, *be prepared coming in to start planning for the day when you will be getting out.* Before taking over, develop a timeline for mentoring your chosen successor in the job with a series of goals. As you recall from the introduction, Nick's dad never considered an exit strategy and had no desire for one because he never intended to relinquish control. So when ill health physically forced him to step down, he continued to keep his paws on the pulse of the business, subverting his son's every effort to change management philosophy and direction and to improve employee morale.

Insider Tip #7

How you enter the business and how you leave it are connected. The degree to which you understand and honor this connection will determine how successful you are as a CEO.

You can learn something from every person
you meet—even if it's what not to do.

—**Abraham Lincoln**

The father buys, the son builds, the
grandchild sells, and his son begs.

—**Scottish Proverb**

Pride and Pressure

Carrying On the Family Legacy

In my early days as CEO, I felt enormous pressure to succeed. I had been handed a business that two men had devoted their entire lives to building, and I had to do right by them, my entire family, all our employees, and Arkay's many loyal customers. As if that weren't enough stress, I knew that the odds were stacked against me: third-generation owners notoriously fail to sustain, let alone grow, their family businesses.

My need to prove my worthiness—especially to my dad and to myself—often prevented me from viewing business matters objectively. Consequently, I made plenty of mistakes. I decided, though, that quitting wasn't an option—regardless of the number of times I wanted to throw my hands in the air and yell, "I'm outta here!"

I learned many lessons from my leadership transition, not just from making mistakes but also from occasionally scoring a touchdown. As you take the helm of a family business, these lessons can help you make smart decisions and keep your company thriving—even as you juggle the complex emotional and psychological demands that come with your new position.

Must Bring Data

What doesn't get measured doesn't get improved. We can apply that wisdom to almost anything—but especially to business.

When taking over a company, you need to appreciate the significance of those words or you may start off having a negative impact instead of the positive one you intend.

It took me some time on the job before I realized that being in the dark about any key area of the business (sales, operations, or finance)—that is, not knowing where it stood *in the moment*—could threaten opportunities for progress in that area and jeopardize the future of the company. I had to learn this the hard way.

By nature, I'm a fairly trusting person, generally believing what my team tells me. During my early days as leader, when my chief financial officer told me something, I didn't doubt him—particularly since it spared me the hassle of digging into financial matters myself. My strengths coming into the business lay more in sales and marketing than in finances. I liked and excelled at both of them, so of course that's where I wanted to put all my attention.

People generally tell you what you want to hear—especially if you give off vibes that you want them to. And, boy, did I give off those vibes! If my CFO delivered bad news, I'd get so angry that I'd lash out at him—unprofessional, not to mention unproductive. That kind of response doesn't exactly encourage your CFO to continue being honest. It didn't take long for mine to get that message and start doing the opposite. He sugarcoated everything rather than risk my wrath by revealing what was really happening.

> Eventually, I learned to analyze and question what I was being told and to accept the truth, whether I liked it or not, without blowing off steam.

This went on until I began noticing inconsistencies between what he was saying and what I was seeing with my own eyes. Knowing I couldn't operate with someone I couldn't trust, I forced myself to take control of the finances of the business, just as I should have from the beginning. Eventually, I learned to analyze and question what I was being told and to accept the truth, whether I liked it or not, without blowing off steam.

Assuming a leadership role, however, does not translate into trying to do everything yourself. On the contrary, you should surround yourself with people whose expertise exceeds yours in their particular field. You must first pinpoint your weak areas— one of the guidelines I introduced in chapter 1—and then stay open to learning as much about them as you can so you can *lead* your expert team more effectively.

As I mentioned, it took quite a while for all this to sink in and for me to see how having current information—and the capability and willingness to evaluate it properly and unemotionally— affects the ability of any business to advance. To give you an idea of just how long it took, a professor of mine at Rochester Institute of Technology named John Compton first told me about the connection between what gets measured and what gets improved. He specialized in statistical process control (SPC): measuring and developing standard operating procedures for quality-improvement initiatives in technology businesses like mine. He lived by the mantra "In God we trust. All others must bring data." And so should you.

Insider Tip #8

Shooting all the messengers won't change the facts. To create a healthy working environment and position your company for success, you must welcome all the news—the good and the bad— and review data objectively.

Smelling the Trends

When my father was running Arkay back in 1974, seven unions on Long Island, New York, where our facilities were located, went on strike. They demanded a 40 percent increase over eighteen months for their workers. My dad had to go head-to-head with all seven unions, resulting in a very stressful and turbulent two and a half years of negotiations. As the discussions wore on, even the tires on people's cars were slashed.

A brave group of local high school students crossed the picket lines to work for us (some are still with us today, like Walter J. Shiels, our COO), despite having their lives threatened by angry picketers. One even felt a gun pushed into the small of his back while he was in the bathroom at a local restaurant, and the gunman told him that he should quit scabbing if he wanted to continue breathing.

> It didn't take much of a nose to smell a trend here—my gut feeling told me that if we stayed on Long Island, the cost of doing business would soon put us *out* of business.

Finally, the strike ended, and my dad was victorious in eliminating six of the unions, losing out to only one: the printers' union.

Fast-forward more than twenty years. Now I was in the hot seat. The wage increases kept coming with no end in sight. Meanwhile, with advancements in technology, our competitors were catching up with us and taking market share. It didn't take much of a nose to smell a trend here—my gut feeling told me that if we stayed on Long Island, the cost of doing business would soon put us *out* of business.

So almost as soon as I succeeded to CEO, I began searching for more business-friendly locations to build a plant, like Mexico, Florida, Georgia, Kentucky, Pennsylvania, North Carolina, or Virginia. The South seemed a bright spot for us, and we looked seriously in that direction. Virginia's governor at the time, George Allen, strongly supported manufacturing. He offered us attractive incentives to move to his state, including free land to build on, an industrial revenue bond for $10 million dollars at 4 percent interest, and an additional $165,000 for relocation and hiring.

Electricity on Long Island was expensive for us. We were spending more than $1 million annually at sixteen cents a kilowatt-hour just to power the plant—in addition to all our other expenses like taxes, payroll, and medical costs. In Virginia, electricity cost four cents a kilowatt-hour—a big savings right there. The game was changing, and new rules were coming into play. Among them was the necessity to become a lower-cost supplier, a significant trend affecting not just our business but many others as well.

A good number of my friends who used to manufacture have essentially become importers, either representing factories or owning parts of factories in China because of its generally low production costs. They told me that to stay competitive, Arkay would have to start making its cartons in China too. Despite their admonitions, I didn't see this particular trend as a legitimate threat. Still, I decided to visit the economic behemoth anyway to get an up-close view of my own.

In 2002, I flew to Taipei, Hong Kong, Guangdong, and Shanghai to check out the most respected packaging companies that served our industry. Pleasantly surprised, I found that every one of them had slow-running equipment and that the cartons were still being die cut, stamped, and glued by hand, which is incredibly labor intensive. On the other hand, Arkay's equipment is fast and highly automated, enabling us to counterbalance costs through technology efficiencies.

I repeated my Far East trip in 2006 to see what might have changed and was happy again with my findings. China now has its own pricing challenges as an exporter because of more stringent environmental requirements, six-day workweeks, overtime, longer lead times, mandatory health care on the horizon, and higher export taxes.

Choosing to follow my instincts, I began laying the groundwork for building a manufacturing plant in Virginia, where we've been now for fourteen years. In anticipating the threat of continuing to be a high-cost provider in a competitive industry, we built a plant in a less-expensive, employer-friendly state, rather than joining the stampede and moving all the way to China.

Insider Tip #9

Family businesses often get mired down in the status quo—but to stay vibrant, companies must constantly evolve. When you assume leadership, trust your intuition to point you in new directions.

Friend Today, Enemy Tomorrow

In the 1970s, Arkay supplied folding cartons to the Japanese cosmetics giant Shiseido. In today's dollars, we did $8 million annually with them. They demanded the highest quality possible and we delivered. Shiseido loved us—or so we thought.

One day a spokesperson for a group of affiliated Japanese manufacturers called to ask if they could visit our plant. My father said yes. Proud of our facility, he loved showing people around. The twelve Japanese visitors wanted to know if they could take photos, and my father, an amateur photographer, said sure. They bowed and started shooting away. After the tour and all the requisite pleasantries, they bowed again and left. Within a couple of weeks, my father received a thank-you gift from them: an impressive glass-enclosed stuffed owl, probably costing several thousand dollars, to add to the owl collection they had noticed in his office.

A year later, Shiseido pulled all its business away. The company executives offered no explanation other than that they were going elsewhere. Where to? It didn't take much guessing—to one of the affiliated Japanese manufacturers who had visited.

We still have the owl in the office to remind us never to allow anyone to photograph our operations again.

I experienced a similar situation in 1995 with an outsourcing partner we had chosen. With our sales up 38 percent over the previous year, we had been struggling to support our delivery criteria. To stem the bleeding and get back on track, I turned for help to a packaging firm that made chipboard packer boxes mostly for customers in the golf ball industry.

To finalize our short-term arrangement, I met the owner at a

> Sure enough, as soon as the noncompete expired, he hired one of my former salesmen and started going directly after my core customers. Today, he is one of my main competitors.

printing industry event he was hosting at his factory. The irony of the story is that after I visited his facility, he told me he was worried about my viewing his plant because he wasn't sure he could trust me. I was concerned as well, so I requested that he sign a noncompete agreement, which named specific customers within a specific time frame. When he started completing orders for them, I became more apprehensive because he hadn't previously produced value-added packaging. Indeed, was he a rival in the making?

Once I cleaned up our delivery issues, I stopped utilizing him. Sure enough, as soon as the noncompete expired, he hired one of my former salesmen and started going directly after my core customers. Today, he is one of my main competitors.

Here is yet another example from my early days as a CEO:

Over the years that my father was running Arkay, most of the press equipment manufacturers in America were bought up by German companies. Our primary equipment came from Germany and our finishing equipment from Switzerland. My father traveled across the pond every four years for unveilings of the latest technology innovations at the number one printing trade show in the world in Düsseldorf, Germany.

I would frequently go with him, and we became quite friendly with the owners of several family-owned businesses in the folding-carton trade. As amiable overseas competitors, we would share ideas on technology and other topics while dining on *spargel* (German asparagus) homegrown in their gardens. We gave plant tours to one another and Arkay even hired the son of one owner to intern for a summer.

I continued this Good Neighbor Policy even when I assumed leadership and began calling on all our major customers to make sure we were delivering on their expectations. At one of those accounts, as we were concluding our business, the senior executive looked at me in a serious, but caring way and cautioned me, "Mitchell, be careful. The Germans are coming!" All the air went out of me as I realized exactly what he was driving at: our close overseas friends of so many years, with whom we had shared so much, were intent on coming after our core customers and business *on our shores* in the new global economy.

Even though I had known about the earlier incident involving the Japanese, it apparently hadn't altogether stuck with me, for here was history repeating itself, this time with an offshore competitor. Never again would this happen, I said to myself then—and it hasn't.

Insider Tip #10

Remember that projecting your good intentions on rivals can yield unsavory results: a friend today could easily turn into a competitor tomorrow.

Consistency is King

Since the beginning of my tenure as CEO of Arkay, I have championed for dependably high product-quality scores and levels of service: my number one rule of success. The only way to accomplish this is by establishing measurements. You can have the best intentions to meet a goal, but without ways of quantifying achievement each day, month, and year, you have no way of gauging your progress. Many new successor-owners may find few such practices in place due to a long-standing culture of handling everything with just a nod and a handshake.

McDonald's is probably one of the most famous organizations noted for their product and service consistency throughout the world. No matter where you are—Miami, Los Angeles,

Paris, Hong Kong, or Rome—a Big Mac tastes the same. The ingredients, sauce, and presentation all come down to an exact science. Franchise owners even attend McDonald's Hamburger University to learn how to use measurement tools to maintain consistent procedures, quality, and service.

In contrast, when I took over Arkay, our culture was dominated by inconsistencies: in product- and service-quality measurements, standard operating procedures, and a disciplined approach to communication. Some days we were rock stars with our top customers, while other days we were on "double secret probation."

As the first step toward correcting the situation, we determined how to apply the concept of measurement to our operations. For example, prompt deliveries are critical to a business like ours whose customers have scheduled launches of new products all the time. How do you achieve 100 percent on-time delivery without knowing where you are? So we started tracking the numbers and found we were hitting about 30 percent. A shocking discovery, but the data didn't lie.

Some days we were rock stars with our top customers, while other days we were on "double secret probation."

The only place to go was up. To get there, we had to define *exactly* what "on-time" meant. We started defining it as "seven days late to seven days early" and then as "six days late to six days early," reducing the number of days until we finally reached "dock date and in-full delivery of products." After establishing measurements for consistency and accountability for accomplishing it, we found that our on-time delivery soared to an average of 95 to 100 percent with *all* our customers.

Injecting discipline into the organization was job number two. Without it, no activity or results can be consistent. Just as long-distance runners must commit to their training and diet to repeatedly win marathons, businesses must commit to sound policies to achieve long-term vitality.

Because Arkay's productivity and success depends on constant communication among our multiple facilities, we began scheduling regular morning meetings to review everything from the previous night's shipping to billing achievements, and to set clear-cut objectives for the upcoming day—a practice that continues today. I insist that everyone attending these meetings come prepared to accomplish something specific, make an important decision, or agree on a new direction or procedure—all necessary actions for improving and maintaining consistency in every area of the business.

Insider Tip #11

To revitalize and grow your company, eliminate generations-old informal and erratic practices. Discipline plus empowerment plus accountability equals progress.

Achieving Financial Consistency

Many people's lives rest on a CEO's decisions and ability to remain in the black. But it is very difficult to demonstrate steady financial results when your day-to-day business is constantly fluctuating.

When I took over Arkay in the 1990s, we were known as the finest value-added packaging company in the world. But as I mentioned, competition had become so fierce that making money was not as easy as it had been in the 1960s and '70s. Back then, even if a quality problem forced us to redo a job, we could still realize a profit on it. Today, on the other hand, we have little to no wiggle room. We have to be absolutely on schedule or we could lose money on an order.

To ensure we stayed on plan, I decided when I assumed control that even though we were a privately held business, I would share all critical financial information with my team of managers. This decision grew out of my overall business philosophy to take fiduciary responsibility and reduce the pattern of making, losing, and then making money again. Every month, we set budgets and hold meetings to openly discuss the specifics of each manager's area of responsibility. Such transparency, diligent oversight, and mutual trust have helped us keep our competitive edge.

Insider Tip #12

Make transparency an integral part of your business culture. It is essential to achieving financial consistency.

WEEKLY SCORECARDS

My friend and colleague Scott Levy is also in the printing business and has four manufacturing plants in four different states. To monitor them and evaluate how they're doing in the top metric areas of quality level, on-time delivery, sales, safety, and so on, he relies on what he calls Weekly Balance Scorecards. He lists all key points on a one-page docu-  ment for each employee, team, and plant. It is an excellent way to grade performance and accountability.

As soon as Scott recommended this measuring tool to me, I began using it to help create consistency out of chaos. You should use it too, regardless of your type of business. You will be amazed at how quickly everyone in your organization starts focusing on achieving.

Surround yourself with the very best
people, and spend a lot of time trying
to create a common sense of purpose.

—**Stanley O'Neal**

THREE

You With Me or Against Me?
Building a Loyal Team

Having two quarterbacks on the field will spell disaster. Although my dad said he'd stay out of the day-to-day operations once I officially took over Arkay, he'd still show up and run some plays, often while I was away on a business trip. The team would then wonder which one of us was in charge. Leadership must be clearly defined; otherwise, the players will be confused in their loyalties and unreceptive to the successor's goals.

When I became president and CEO of Arkay, I acquired a management team whose allegiance was understandably 95 percent to my father, and it was hard for many to adjust. A newcomer—whether family member or hired gun—is frequently viewed as an outsider and a threat. My dad's continued involvement made the transition even more difficult for several of the managers and for me as I tried to determine who shared my vision and who needed to be replaced.

Some members of the existing team were respectful and immediately loyal to me. Others couldn't—or wouldn't—accept me in my new role. Some were very capable in their particular area of responsibility, but others were less so. And some were open and receptive to new ideas and change, while others remained stubbornly attached to the outdated ways, using rumor mongering and nay-saying to sabotage my efforts to modernize.

Cleaning House

As one of my first orders of business, I had to eliminate what I called the cancerous people, those who infected every meeting with their negativity. Whenever a new idea was proposed, they'd say "It won't work" or "It can't be done," and do their best to recruit others into their defeatist camp. Don't get me wrong. If I make a suggestion and overlook its downside, I want to know. What I don't want is a pervasive attitude of "not possible." I need members of my staff to keep their pessimism to themselves—or look for another job.

As one of my first orders of business, I had to eliminate what I called the cancerous people, those who infected every meeting with their negativity.

It took me a long time to build my own management team, especially since I was analyzing who was who and what was what, and who should stay and who should go while actively performing my duties as a CEO. This is why you must evaluate how your team operates and determine how many direct reports you have (versus how many you should have) *before* starting the job.

The military has always led by chain of command. When lives are on the line, soldiers must go through the proper channels to act measurably and with speed and purpose. At Arkay, we have made leading from the top down by chain of command work effectively for us. As in the military, managers have clearly defined areas of responsibility and know exactly where to go to get something approved.

We have also flattened out our organizational structure as much as possible to eliminate layers of unproductive bureaucracy. By doing so, we have developed a great deal of trust within the organization. We all have a sense of being our own boss. Everyone benefits. Micromanaging goes out the window, and people feel truly empowered. If your type of business allows it, I highly recommend moving in this flatter direction.

> ## Insider Tip #13
>
> You will undoubtedly feel overwhelmed with the tasks of your new position, so take time before assuming control to fully evaluate the skills and values of working family members and the other personnel awaiting you.

Making Judgment Calls

How do you determine good versus bad when building your team? Remember it's all about being a *member* of the team, not being the top dog. Egos need to be left at the door. I assess how valuable players are by how well they work with others over the course of a year. I've sometimes had to let go of the superstars who felt they were above the rules and agreements put in place. When hiring a new team member, you need to keep certain pre-requisites in mind.

What to Look For

Knowing your strengths and weaknesses will prove very helpful here. It opens the door to determining what special abilities you will need from others to balance yours so you can do your job more effectively. This is your secret weapon in building a team.

For example, my executive assistant is one of the most important people on my team. Because I'm not especially organized, she must possess superb organizational skills. To enable me to direct my attention and energies as much as possible on my strengths (sales and marketing), my executive assistant coordinates speaking engagements, customer appointments, and company meetings, as well as handling my travel arrangements and managing all my correspondence. That way, I can focus solely on the doing.

I also look for people who share my values. Here are the most important:

- A passion for the company and a desire to see it succeed

- An attitude of never surrendering when things get tough, of working harder and staying positive

- The courage to confront brutal facts and make the tough decisions for the greater good

- The willingness to be accountable and follow through on commitments

- The ability to celebrate as a team when we win and not blame others when we don't

Where to Look

I don't want to give the impression that everyone on the existing team when I took over Arkay from my father was a bad fit. Far from it. I found many skilled people whose values and qualities aligned perfectly with mine. I also discovered that some of those great employees had just been in the wrong position and that a change brought out the best in them.

Promoting from within, rather than immediately looking outside the company to build my team, was an early—and instrumental—accomplishment of mine. Looking inside your organization for talent will generally produce a much higher "batting average" in your rate of successful hiring.

Insider Tip #14

Your company's health will dictate whether you need to keep anyone from the previous team or start from scratch. Don't rush the decision process—but don't take too long either—and stay open to changing course if you realize you've made a wrong decision.

Surviving the Perfect Storm: A Case Study

There is no greater test of teammates than a crisis. Do they step up to the plate, or do they panic, start playing the blame game, run and hide—or quit? As with romantic relationships, it's easy to stick around when things are going well, but what happens when problems come knocking and you hit some rough spots?

In my early days as CEO, my top managers (most of them still with me today) and I lived through a perfect storm of trouble. The highly stressful experience really tested our mettle and our respective loyalties, trust, and confidence.

The clouds first started forming when I made the decision to build a new plant in Roanoke, Virginia, and move some of our printing there. As I explained in chapter 2, I was eager to offset the high labor and other costs of doing business in Long Island, our home base.

We began construction in early 1995 and went into production the following year. Building a major manufacturing facility some 500 miles away and getting it up and running in so short a time are no simple tasks. Fortunately, the annual snowfall in that part of Virginia typically averages three to four inches a year. That year, however, the blizzard of the century blew in, dropping more than four feet of snow while we were under pressure to complete construction in record time.

> That year, however, the blizzard of the century blew in, dropping more than four feet of snow while we were under pressure to complete construction in record time.

Just prior to breaking ground for the new plant, we bought a smaller printing company on Long Island called Grinnell Lithograph. Its central customers included Clairol, Warner Lambert, and Häagen-Dazs ice cream. This was a sales-purchase agreement—only a few key employees, two pieces of equipment, and the accounts. No investment bankers or brokers were involved—just a simple transaction with the potential of adding a great deal to Arkay's bottom line.

But it was too good to be true. As the whiteout hit Virginia, the clouds in our perfect storm grew very dark. It turned out that Clairol had been considering moving its business away from the Grinnell operation for some time. Fourteen months after our purchase, as snow was falling in Virginia, Clairol opted to take a hike, departing with millions of dollars in anticipated business.

Just when we thought our storm couldn't get worse, the Environmental Protection Agency (EPA) came after us for installing a huge label press before obtaining the proper permit. My father had decided that as his last hurrah in the business, he would purchase a prototype label press he had had his eye on and had even contributed to developing. We all thought a "one-stop shopping" concept would interest our packaging customers since many of them also bought labels for their primary components. The machine was huge and promised to do everything.

The EPA fined us $25,000 for our violation. Because this was my dad's baby, he was outraged.

"That's highway robbery!" he shouted. "I refuse to pay it."

So we took the EPA to court.

But they don't like companies fighting back. Our negotiations with them broke down. And then our perfect storm finally hit full force when the local newspaper, Long Island's *Newsday*, got wind of the story. I was on the way out of my office, headed for a dinner engagement, when I got the call.

"Hello, this is Mitchell Kaneff, how can I help you?" I asked.

"I'm calling from *Newsday*," the voice said. "Would you care to comment on your current fines and pending litigation with the EPA?"

"No," I said and hung up.

The next day I got calls, one right after the other, from my executive vice president and my receptionist asking me if I'd seen the morning issue of *Newsday*. Since I lived in Manhattan and didn't subscribe, I said, "No, why?"

They said they'd fax the article over to me. Moments later, I read in big black letters, **"Hauppauge Printer Pollutes!"** At the time, Elliot Spitzer (now the infamous ex-governor of New York) was a lawyer running for New York State attorney general. He was quoted in *Newsday* as saying, "We won't tolerate polluters like Arkay on Long Island." The article went on to claim that the attorney general was seeking a fine of $60 million.

Many of our competitors faxed the piece to our top customers, who besieged us with phone calls, asking us in a panic whether we were filing Chapter 11 or Chapter 7. The power of print is unbelievable! To stop the bleeding, we quickly put together a letter reassuring everyone that (as Mark Twain might say) rumors of our death were highly exaggerated. All our critical accounts stayed with us except one. But the bleeding could have been a helluva lot worse.

We hired an environmental attorney to fight the EPA, but at the end of the day, we spent over $300,000 in legal fees and wound up settling anyway. We also paid a $150,000 fine for the violation we'd incurred installing the label machine without getting the proper permit. If we had just paid the $25,000 fine early on, we would have saved ourselves $425,000—and a lot of aggravation. Sometimes it's better to cut your losses, even if the charge seems unjust.

We learned many hard lessons. Chief among them were (1) don't bite off more than you can chew at any one time; (2) don't try to fight city hall—the government always wins; and (3) the media is extremely powerful and often quite manipulative, so never ignore the press—talk to reporters when they contact you and choose your words carefully.

Most importantly, though, we learned that we had a top-flight team in place, from management and operations to human resources and public relations. If we could survive that kind of perfect storm, with everything hitting us at once, we could survive anything. And I discovered that I had a dedicated, passionate team capable of seeing me through every difficulty—even one of my own making.

A decade later, Arkay faced yet another dire situation, one that especially tested my management team. Among other offenses, I discovered that my CFO had been lying to everyone—bankers, vendors, and me—about the company's finances (the second of two disreputable CFOs I've worked with!). At that time, he belonged to a loosely grouped-together core of executives, including Walt Shiels, Brian Hopkins, and Darlene Triglia.

Because of the CFO's antics, not only had we lost all credibility with our bankers, but we had also developed a serious negative cash flow problem that threatened the company's future. I had no choice but to fire him. Fortunately, this single act helped reinstate Arkay's standing with the banking community.

It also coalesced the remaining executives. Prior to the disaster, the team was one in name only. Although committed and hardworking, all the members were doing their own thing—they didn't share a genuine connection. But the CFO crisis allowed a bonding to take place, which has only grown progressively stronger in the ensuing years. The banks said our recovery was the fastest they had ever witnessed, and the support and loyalty of my newly crystallized team made going through that storm an apex in my professional life.

Insider Tip #15

If a weak link exists within your core leadership team, you must remove the individual—or the integrity, resolve, and strength of the entire team will be irrevocably compromised.

If you want to go fast, go alone. If you want to go far, go with others.

—**African Proverb**

FOUR

Somebody to Lean On
Looking Outside for Help

While working on this book, I read in the *Wall Street Journal* about William Lauder's decision to step down (or "abdicate," according to the article) from being CEO, the position he'd held for almost a decade as leader of the Estée Lauder Companies.

Lauder offered this reason for leaving: "Leading a public company is a sentence, but leading a publicly held, family-controlled business is a life sentence. I didn't want to be taken out of here feet first." He revealed that he had been "beset by family members with differing agendas, long hours, and fighting the perception that his success [was] only due to his legendary last name."

The piece went on to describe the Lauders as a "classic tale of the generational tensions that so often surround a family business. There's the son struggling to live up to his father's legacy, the powerhouse father who keeps close tabs on the empire, and a high-profile, big-spending uncle."[1]

Although I tend not to believe everything I read in the newspaper (rightly so, given the media's coverage of our battle with the EPA), I happen to know William Lauder personally and completely understand his perspective. It can, indeed, be very lonely at the top. That's true of every leadership position, of course. But it seems to be especially true for those of us who ascend to

---

1. Ellen Byron, "Tensions Roil Estée Lauder Dynasty," *Wall Street Journal*, February 27, 2008, http://online.wsj.com/article/SB120406413598194599.html.

the "throne" of a large, long-standing, and successful family operation. Not only are we called on to make the typical business decisions all CEOs must make, but we must do so amid sometimes-turbulent family dynamics and with a spotlight that can often seem quite harsh. The previous leader may not welcome our efforts to expose the unpleasant realities about the business and about family employees. These dual challenges can place an enormous burden on successors, or as I (and Lauder) sometimes put it, lead to their leaving the job "feet first."

My family and I have often described ourselves as putting the "dys" into "dysfunctional." Yet we have always managed to resolve the difficulties that everyone (notably my dad) has had about my role in the company. I attribute this to our collective ability to talk things through—nonstop communication has been our guiding refrain. Other CEOs and their families, though, can often find these problems insurmountable, especially if successors allow themselves to be governed by an "I can (or must) do it myself" mentality.

Those of us who assume control of a family-held company, with rare exception, have never done it before, and we must equip ourselves emotionally to navigate this unfamiliar territory. Under these circumstances, it is by no means an admission of failure or weakness to want to seek guidance from consultants when making personal as well as professional decisions. At some point in the transition process, we all need a coach or a mentor, someone who can help us cut through the fog of family or business issues (or both at the same time) with some sound ad-

> **At some point in the transition process, we all need a coach or a mentor, someone who can help us cut through the fog of family or business issues (or both at the same time) with some sound advice.**

vice. To find the best, most appropriate help, we need to uncover and access all our options.

Support in Many Forms

Professional consultants are available to provide counsel (for a fee, of course) on everything from sales and marketing to employee relations to plant design. For free advice on business or personal matters, an industry group, a professional organization of peers, or an outside board can be excellent resources. Don't overlook them.

For example, a friend of mine owns an auto parts business, and at one time, he had manufacturing facilities in both the United States and China. A few years ago, he was struggling with declining margins, excessive overhead, and fading profits from his U.S. division. He wasn't sure if he needed to sell or merge the business to survive. The situation was tearing him apart.

As the crisis was coming to a head, my friend joined the Young Presidents' Organization (YPO), an international group of presidents and CEOs under the age of forty-nine. To help members become "better leaders through education and idea exchange," the organization encourages them to take advantage of the YPO Forum. Most YPOers would agree that participating in this activity is a tremendously valuable experience and one of the best rewards of their membership.

The YPO Forum serves as a cure for the isolation chief executives often feel. Lasting four hours, each meeting offers a safe environment for discussing and obtaining multiple viewpoints on important and confidential business—as well as on personal and family-related concerns—from people who have "been there." As stated in the YPO brochure (see www.ypo.org),

Young business leaders need somewhere to turn for the insight
and perspective only a true peer can provide. In YPO, that place
is Forum. . . . Today, there are more than 1,500 Forums around
the world providing members with a place where they can share
openly without concern that what they discuss will reverberate
in their businesses, families, or communities.

After attending several forum meetings, my troubled friend
in the auto parts business gained much-needed clarity and advice from fellow YPOers, many of whom had faced a similar
"sell or merge" decision. The back-and-forth group therapy
helped him confront the brutal fact that the exorbitant labor
costs at his U.S. plant were weighing down his company. To stay
in business, he had to outsource all his manufacturing to his
China operation. So he chose to shut down the U.S. facility and
sell the property rather than merge with another company and
lose control. The YPO Forum then helped him lay out and address the issues involved in restructuring his business.

Today, my friend is a much happier man, and his company is
flourishing. Of course, he was the one who had to make the final
decisions. The group just lent him support. But it was his willingness to stay open and listen instead of falling prey to the "I can
do it myself" syndrome that enabled him to seek guidance when
he needed it.

The Consultant's Role

The primary tasks of outside advisors are to *listen* to you and *understand* your values and priorities so they can help you perform
your duties more effectively during the transition. A consultant
can also pinpoint your special talents and determine whether

you're able to fully apply them to the job. Perhaps you have been spending your time doing other, less productive things. An advisor can then customize a game plan that will ultimately allow you to focus more of your time on those activities requiring your particular abilities.

In my business, consultants have proved particularly useful when facilitating projects like these:

- Designing training programs, such as apprenticeships for next-level manufacturing or sales teams

- Developing standard operating procedures for reducing tremendous volumes of paperwork and simplifying data retrieval

- Creating contingency plans (for example, fire, insurance, and police protection; and alternate manufacturing facilities)

- Preparing budgets and profit plans

- Mapping out long-range strategies

- Building teams: fostering trust, accountability, and vision sharing

When using consultants for these purposes, you must clearly define goals, expectations, a measurable time frame, and a reasonable, set price. Otherwise, the problem for which the consultant is hired could linger on unsolved for years, costing you a fortune, as the consultant becomes a fixture in your organization. In other words, *know when to cut the cord.*

For example, during my transition as CEO, I brought in a consultant early on to help me with leadership issues. I suspect that my insecurities associated with taking on a big new role along with trying to fill the shoes of my father, the industry legend, made me rely too heavily on the consultant's guidance and not enough on my own instincts. When I realized during a strategy meeting that I wasn't running it—he was—I knew the time had come for me to dismiss him. He was taking things in a direction I didn't agree with. I couldn't blame him. *I had allowed it to happen.* But I needed to reclaim my company.

My advisor had helped me achieve sufficient leadership strength and determination to perform the job. He had accomplished what I had hired him to do, but I had to let him go before he became a crutch. That is why you must have an exit strategy when working with consultants.

I expressed my thanks and said good-bye.

Insider Tip #16

With all the stresses of transitioning into a family business, you could easily hang on to outside advisors too long. Cut them loose—even though you feel like you're free-falling. If they helped you once, you can always hire them again.

Industrial Psychologists

Industrial psychologists are like marriage counselors, except that they help owners and managers of businesses improve the quality of the workplace, solve particular problems, and identify ways to achieve success. For family-owned organizations, these professionals help successor CEOs and their relatives handle the complex, tense interactions that all too frequently crop up and wreak havoc. Take my situation, for example.

Before I came in, my father had run the business his way, on his own, answering to no one. Then all of a sudden—*Whack! Pow! Boom!*—like a scene from the old *Batman* TV series, he was saddled with a partner who also happened to be his still-wet-behind-the-ears offspring and thirty-plus years his junior. My dad and I had always gotten along personally, but we had to figure out how to relate to each other professionally in a super-charged new environment, one in which he would ultimately pass me the baton. Sometimes, even though leaders of a company say they are ready to do this, they really aren't. This was the case with my father.

Fortunately, we both agreed to address the challenges we had with each other by consulting with an industrial psychologist I'll call Sam. I formed an immediate kinship with him and wanted the process to move along as quickly as possible. However, my father bobbed and weaved, and was inclined toward dragging it out. Although he and I eventually worked through our problems, it took far longer than I would have liked.

I highly recommend going into each session with the objective of establishing—under the guidance of the industrial psychologist—some follow-up steps to keep pushing the transition forward rather than leaving the meetings too open-ended. We all have the ability to forget commitments and regress, so I urge you to take notes on what is agreed upon.

Sometimes, the discussions my dad and I had during these sessions became quite heated. I remember one in particular involving a book of key action items I had put together to assist him with the company. When I gave it to him with the intention of helping him in specific areas, he was offended—not by the contents but by the fact that the book had come from me. In his mind, my suggestions were tantamount to criticism and therefore completely unacceptable to him.

For family-owned organizations, these professionals help successor CEOs and their relatives handle the complex, tense interactions that all too frequently crop up and wreak havoc.

On occasion, our disagreements escalated into full-blown shouting matches. We even walked away from one another a few times. Sam was there, though, to help us over the rough spots, and as I've said, my dad and I have always had a strong relationship.

Sam also helped me realize—and, more importantly, face up to—what was really eating away at me: As much as I loved my dad and wanted him to stay in the business, his presence seriously disrupted my management of the company. He was preventing me from taking Arkay in the new direction I thought best.

In 2004, the situation finally reached a crisis point the morning after I arrived in Las Vegas for leadership training meetings with my YPO Forum group. The phone rang early in my hotel room, jolting me awake. My COO was calling from New York. "Mitchell, I just can't take it anymore," he said. "I'm going to have to resign." I told him to calm down, take a deep breath, and tell me what was happening, assuring him I'd work things out.

At our last session with Sam, just before I went out of town, my dad and I had negotiated some rules concerning his interactions with the members of my executive team: in other words, he would not interfere with them. And yet I wasn't even out of town one day before he was back running the company, ordering my senior staff to come into his office and take notes on his ideas regarding—it didn't matter what it was regarding because my team had had enough! And so had I. That was the last straw. Things had to change—dramatically.

Furious, I immediately called my dad and yelled into the phone that either he was leaving Arkay or I was. I refused to let him continue hijacking my authority. "You can buy back the shares of the company from me and run it and I'll leave to do something else," I told him, "or you can play in my sandbox under the rules we all agreed to." He was silent on the other end. I hung up the phone.

Not sure exactly what to do, I discussed the problem with my YPO Forum mates later that morning. "You've got to get rid of him," one member advised me. "Offer him a new position as chairman emeritus."

The idea made sense to me and I confirmed it with Sam. I decided to write a letter to my father terminating his employment at Arkay. I composed it on the plane flying home and called my dad as soon I landed to tell him we had to meet right away. This was probably the most difficult decision I've ever had to make, but my mind was made up.

When we met, I presented him with the letter on the following page. After he read it, he hugged me. As tears welled up in my eyes, he thanked me for stepping up to the plate. He said he wasn't upset with me—on the contrary, he said he was very proud of me and acknowledged that I was right: it was time for him to leave. I had been president of Arkay since 1997 but it was not until that moment in 2004 that I became the company's actual leader. The transition was made final.

Sam was instrumental in helping me take this painful, but necessary action. Soon afterward, I let him go, occasionally calling him for a session or two as the need arose.

April 4, 2004

Dear Dad,

I love, respect, and admire you. You developed a reputation as one of the finest value-added folding-carton companies in the world. You have been an industry leader, a pioneer, and an innovator, and I'm grateful for everything you have done and given me.

This letter is the one of the hardest I have ever written, but I know it will ultimately strengthen our relationship, even though you may not think so now. I've begun a new chapter in my life, and the time has come for me to take full responsibility and ownership of Arkay.

My goal is to create a great company. I will accomplish this by delivering my vision, defining clear objectives, remaining focused, and instilling discipline. In order for me to succeed, one voice needs to be heard at the top of the organization.

So effective immediately, I will be taking over as chairman and CEO, and I'm appointing you to the prestigious position of chairman emeritus. I see your role as my confidant as well as my consigliere.

My job is to increase our shareholder value, strengthen our balance sheet, improve our EBITDA, and generate positive cash flow. Making money for our company is my primary goal! I will also design a plan to pay you back your $3 million dollars of subordinated debt.

I need to run this company from strength. I love you and want our relationship to blossom and not decay. I'm asking for your support and blessing.

All great kings retire!

Love,
Mitchell

Author Julia Flynn Siler reveals more-mixed results in her book *The House of Mondavi: The Rise and Fall of an American Wine Dynasty* (Gotham Books, 2007). She reports that, on one hand, the industrial psychologist hired by wine baron Robert Mondavi played a pivotal role in sorting out the myriad—and highly complex—emotional layers of the Mondavi family. Of the therapist's many revelations, the most significant revolved around Mondavi's need to constantly pit one son against the other so he could remain firmly in control of the business.

On the other hand, Flynn Siler writes, this psychologist was so firmly ensconced in the family's graces that when he sat in on board meetings and marketing strategy sessions, Mondavi's staff didn't trust him. Mondavi may have meant well, but he had crossed a line, one that bears mentioning: Good industrial psychologists, however invaluable they may be in succession planning, are first and foremost *family* resources. Their assumption of any other role in that process is almost guaranteed to backfire.

Insider Tip #17

During meetings with industrial psychologists, establish an agenda and follow-up actions to maintain momentum. A succession, like a living organism, must be nurtured—or stagnation will set in.

The Good, the Bad, and the Ugly

As I noted earlier, consultants come in all shapes and sizes, with different skills, personalities, and ways of doing business. Finding an advisor who fits you personally and professionally can pose a real challenge.

The best way to begin your search is by obtaining word-of-mouth referrals. Participate in organizations related to your business to meet people with needs most similar to yours who can be called upon for references. Also, turn to attorneys, tax advisors, and accountants for good leads. Through their work with family-owned businesses, these professionals may know an industrial psychologist who can help you overcome transition hurdles. See appendix B for a list of several sites that offer contact information for advisors throughout the country.

As you find promising consultants, make sure to interview them thoroughly. I once interviewed three qualified candidates for an assignment. Two of them turned out to be duds—I felt no connection at all. But the third had a wonderful, engaging sense of humor that made us click immediately. Guess who got the assignment—and who worked out just as I'd hoped?

I once interviewed three qualified candidates for an assignment. Two of them turned out to be duds—I felt no connection at all.

Of course, this is not to say that possessing a sense of humor is or should be a prerequisite for every candidate, though it often is. I frequently use it as one of the identifiers in the selection process. Yes, the candidate must have all the appropriate credentials for the job. But sensing whether or not you will *enjoy* the process of working with that person is just as important—a key recruitment and interviewing tool that shouldn't be overlooked.

Insider Tip #18

Recruit and interview all potential advisors carefully. The decisions you make jointly will significantly affect your family's future.

When you interview and assess candidates for any type of consulting position, answer this list of questions to help separate out the good, the bad, and the ugly. A "Yes" score of seven or more is a good indicator that the relationship will succeed, especially if the advisor has a sense of humor. Below seven, beware and keep looking.

---

1. Are they tough enough to stand up to you and tell you the harsh facts you may not wish to hear? ❑ Yes ❑ No

2. Are they at least a match in capability for whoever may be currently filling this role for you? ❑ Yes ❑ No

3. Are their rates reasonable and within the industry norms? ❑ Yes ❑ No

4. Can you pin them down to a realistic timeline with an exit strategy? ❑ Yes ❑ No

5. Are they available after business hours or on weekends for emergencies? ❑ Yes ❑ No

6. Do they have a proven track record of success in the assignment area? ❑ Yes ❑ No

7. Are they willing to provide references? ❑ Yes ❑ No

8. Do you have an immediate rapport with them? (Trust your instincts.) ❑ Yes ❑ No

9. Do they listen well and ask probing questions? ❑ Yes ❑ No

10. Are they willing to work in situations in which they may be criticized or not supported by some family members? ❑ Yes ❑ No

I've learned that you can't have everything
and do everything at the same time.

—**Oprah Winfrey**

FIVE

All Work and No Play
Creating a Balance

One of my favorite scary movies of all time is Stanley Kubrick's *The Shining* (1980), based on the novel of the same name by Stephen King. The film has one particular scene that never fails to give me the shivers because it is so subtle, yet so chilling.

The story takes place in an elaborate mountain resort hotel during the off-season. The main character, Jack Torrance (played by Jack Nicholson), has moved there with his wife (Shelley Duvall) and young son (Danny Lloyd) to be the winter caretaker. When not on duty, Torrance, an aspiring writer, spends his time pecking away at an old typewriter on his Great American Novel. As the weeks go by, he begins to get cabin fever and starts acting, shall we say, not quite himself. Meanwhile his wife, beset by fears that someone else may be in the hotel and that her husband may pose a danger to her son, takes to carrying around a baseball bat for protection.

At one point, she enters the room where her husband has been writing and sees his manuscript stacked on the table. A page still sits in the typewriter and she bends down to read it: "All work and no play makes

Jack a dull boy." Turning to the rest of the manuscript, she leafs through and discovers that every page is filled with endless repetitions of the same phrase. She realizes, to her horror, that her husband isn't just suffering from a case of cabin fever but has gone completely round the bend—and that his madness is the source of the danger she has come to fear lurking in the hotel. Topping the scene off, he appears suddenly behind her and asks her opinion of his book: "Well, how do you like it?" And we in the audience jump collectively out of our seats!

Those in business who tend toward "all work and no play" may not go the route of a Jack Torrance and become completely unhinged, but their workaholism most certainly throws their lives out of balance. A friend of mine is a good example. His business does extremely well thanks to his leadership. But the rest of his life has become so far out of whack that as much as he tells me he longs to regain some balance, he has all but forgotten what that looks like. His relationship with his wife is no longer what it was. He has no time for his friends. He gets no exercise. Always in a rush, he succumbs to fast-food dining and has really put on the pounds. Still, he is financially successful; in fact, *Crain's New York Business* magazine has voted him one of the top forty CEOs under age forty in the city.

> His accomplishments have come at an enormous price, however. Suffering from anxiety, he has recently started experiencing panic attacks.

His accomplishments have come at an enormous price, however. Suffering from anxiety, he has recently started experiencing panic attacks. If he doesn't restore some sanity to his life soon, he may not live long enough to enjoy the fruits of his workaholic labors.

Protecting Your Boundaries

The pressures of running a company—regardless of its size—can be daunting enough. But the pressures of running a family-held company can be even more daunting because it's much more difficult to set limits with relatives. A woman I know, whose husband works with his father in the textile industry in North Carolina, told me how her father-in-law calls every night at seven o'clock to talk business with her husband, just as they are sitting down to dinner. He excuses himself to take the call, and she has to keep going into the study to tell him that his dinner is getting cold or that the family is almost finished eating. "It's not just frustrating," she says. "It's *infuriating!*"

> The pressures of running a company—regardless of its size—can be daunting enough. But the pressures of running a family-held company can be even more daunting because it's much more difficult to set limits with relatives.

When his father calls again at seven o'clock, the husband could say to him, "Dad, *after* eight or before seven, I'm all yours. But *between* seven and eight is dinner and family time, and that's sacred, so please don't call." He doesn't say that, though. Because he helps run the family business and the caller is his dad, he has great difficulty safeguarding his boundaries.

Yet to balance work and life, we must be able to do just that. As business leaders, we need our downtime—thinking time, family time, spouse time, and workout time—to keep us from becoming "dull."

Music has always been a big part of my downtime life. I've played bass guitar since I was twelve years old, and I am currently playing bass guitar and recording original music with my rock band, The Young Presidents. For me, the greatest thing about making music is that it enables me to forget about everything else. Whenever I play, I'm fully present and in the moment. This gives me a welcome reprieve from the inevitable headaches at work—a chance to take some deep breaths and clear my head so that when I'm back on the job, I have a much keener, more positive perspective.

Insider Tip #19

You may love your work, but you must get away from it occasionally to return fresher and recharged, especially when you run a family business. How you spend your downtime doesn't matter—as long as you give yourself this gift.

Defining Your Goals

Establishing measurable and attainable goals will go a long way in helping you balance work and life. I have always set them for myself—not just for business but for almost every other aspect of my life as well. I break these nonbusiness goals down into three categories: family, health, and personal. Finding the proper mix takes time, practice, and self-discipline.

Every quarter, I attend a goal-setting workshop sponsored by Strategic Coach (www.strategiccoach.com) in Toronto to aid me with both business and life goals. Founded over twenty years ago, Strategic Coach—with a worldwide clientele from over sixty industries—is unique in that it is run by entrepreneurs, for entrepreneurs. My connection to Strategic Coach has helped me considerably: when you find the right mix, balance becomes second nature.

I may change my goal-setting strategy every quarter, annually, or once every several years. Here's an example of how that "balance equation" might look on paper:

GOALS	
Family	Have dinner at home a minimum of three nights a week
Health	Work out four to six times a week
Personal	Practice guitar one hour each night after kids go to bed

The health aspect of this equation is one of the most important parts for me. By sweating out toxins and releasing stress, I can maintain sufficient energy to go into battle every day and avoid CEO burnout, a common side effect of too little exercise. Constantly faced with making critical decisions in my leadership role, I can't afford that to happen, so I need to squeeze in my workouts as often as possible. Without fail, I must protect this boundary to be able to keep up with the demands of my job.

> By sweating out toxins and releasing stress, I can maintain sufficient energy to go into battle every day and avoid CEO burnout, a common side effect of too little exercise.

To get into a regular workout routine, I recommend beginning with some at-home exercises first thing in the morning after you get out of bed. If you are not a morning person, you may need a little longer to get into this routine but continue to persevere. Studies have shown that it typically takes between twenty-one and twenty-eight days to form a habit, which is essentially what you're trying to do. Give yourself a chance and stay with your exercise program for at least that length of time. Make it part of your schedule by putting it right in your daily calendar. I got so addicted to working out every morning that I now go to a gym six times a week.

If you feel you need additional help to accomplish your health goals, look into hiring a personal trainer for guidance and the push to keep going. Or bring a buddy along to the gym for fun and added support.

Achieving the right balance between your work and home life will be one of the greatest gifts you can give to yourself, to your family, and to the company. It is such a privilege to have this chance to lead—make the most of it.

Insider Tip #20

Struggling to fit work, family, health, and personal activities into your schedule can forever be used as an excuse for not being able to find the time. Don't surrender to procrastination—jump right in!

THE HUMOR QUOTIENT

When you're down, you're never up. The consultant who helped my dad and me turn around our professional relationship greeted me every morning with the following quip if he saw me walk into the office looking discouraged: "Hey, Mitch, every day you're six feet above ground is a good day!" The comment always made me laugh and helped brighten my mood. And at the end of a day, if I happen to go home looking stressed-out, my wife will always say to me, "So, honey, how was your day—bad, horrible, or awful?" This too never fails to make me laugh and lift the heavy weight off my shoulders. Humor is great medicine. Find any way to inject it into your work and your life.

THE GRADITUDE QUOTIENT

Every morning, before I leave home to go to work, I hug and kiss my wife and kids and tell them I love them. It is one way I can show my gratitude for having them in my life. At work, I write down all the busi-

ness victories, large or small, we have achieved since the last quarter or the last year and convey my appreciation to my team. Doing this not only helps me see our progress but also boosts my confidence that we can reach even greater heights.

PLANNING AHEAD

PART 2

He, who every morning plans the transaction of the day and follows out that plan, carries a thread that will guide him through the maze of the most busy life. But where no plan is laid, where the disposal of time is surrendered merely to the chance of incidence, chaos will soon reign.

—Victor Hugo

SIX

The Transition Itinerary
Mapping Out Your Future

This story is true, although the names have been changed to protect the guilty. It is also more common than you might like to think. It is about a father, Dave, and a son, Hank, who ran a family business in New York City that provided printing services to the financial industry on Wall Street. It is the story of how a younger brother, Ricky, became a third partner and altered the family dynamics, forever changing the business. And it is about a younger sister, Sally, who also worked there, but not as a partner, and who got caught in the crossfire.

Dave, the owner-CEO, was a forty-year veteran in the field who knew his clients inside and out. Hank served as his dad's second in command and full partner, a position he had held for about fifteen years. Then Ricky joined the business. After working in the banking industry for several years, he decided he could make more money in the family firm with his contacts than he could on Wall Street.

Upon arriving on the scene, though, Ricky found that although his dad and brother excelled at making money (the business did quite well for all concerned), they paid little attention to how the money was spent—anathema to a bean counter like Ricky. They had no procedures in place—no budgeting process, no financial controls, no future succession strategy. As an equal partner, Ricky wanted his dad and brother to become more aware in these areas. He brought in a consultant to help establish some good practices, triggering anger from his shoot-from-the-hip father and jealousy and resentment from his older brother, a hotshot salesman.

The stage was set for things to turn ugly. And turn ugly they did: Dad and the boys stopped talking to one another. To communicate, they turned to Sally, who was forced into the position of having to listen to all of them vent—just so they could turn against her if she happened to disagree! Eventually she felt so trapped in the middle that she stopped listening and decided to leave, urging them to seek help from an industrial psychologist to smooth things over. But Hank refused. A close friend of his had recently killed himself after going into counseling, thus souring Hank on "shrinks" of any kind forever.

The split within the family finally deteriorated to the point that the company merged with another one on Long Island and

ceased being a family-held entity. Hank had a lifelong passion for sports announcing, so he went into that line of work. Ricky returned to the banking business. Sally moved out of state with her husband, took a job she loved, and never looked back. And not long after the merger, their father died of a heart attack. Some say his premature death was actually due to a broken heart over how things had turned so badly so quickly. And how *everything* he had built had fallen apart—all because roles and expectations had not been clearly defined and a myriad of other challenges had gone unmet. If anyone in the family had thought ahead and worked with the others to develop an effective succession plan, Dave's business might still be thriving today.

Assuming you want your company to continue after you're gone and be just as—and perhaps even more—profitable in the future, the story I just recounted should serve as a wakeup call. It shows why preparing for the next generation of leadership, especially for a family-owned firm, is paramount and why you can't begin the transition process too soon.

A business may have been around for decades under the founder's direction. But that doesn't matter—because longevity doesn't guarantee continued success. Without a strategy in place, a company's long life can end in the blink of an eye. In the case of Arkay, my grandfather Max had a very simple succession plan: he would work until he died. Indeed, he went to sleep one night forty-eight years ago and never woke up. He died a happy man. However, for his successor, my dad, it took many years to rebuild the company and overcome the mistakes my grandfather had made by not planning effectively. Fortunately for us, history did not repeat itself.

> **Longevity doesn't guarantee continued success. Without a strategy in place, a company's long life can end in the blink of an eye.**

Insider Tip #21

Begin succession planning a *minimum* of five to ten years prior to the new leader's taking control. This will provide sufficient time for reviewing and fixing your plan—and some fixing will almost always be needed.

The Starting Point

The goal of succession planning is to achieve—as smoothly as possible—the passing of control and responsibility of the (family) business to the next generation. Based on my experience and seeing firsthand what works and what doesn't, I developed a succession-planning process to help you achieve a positive outcome in your own situation.

Preparing for handing over the reins isn't just a matter of saying to your son or daughter, "When the time comes, we'll just transition you in." On the contrary, you must carefully plan a leadership changeover and avoid making hasty decisions based on single events like illness, marriage, divorce, or death.

I recommend using a process similar to the one you would use when planning a family road trip. Ideally, you would map out an itinerary ahead of time, preparing for contingencies and taking into account everyone participating, including their needs and concerns. The same applies to your transition journey. To optimize your chances of a memorable, hassle-free family vacation or succession, your itinerary must answer these three questions:

1. What are your destinations?

2. What is your timetable?

3. Who is the navigator?

1. What Are Your Destinations?

For your transition journey, I suggest visiting three major areas: leadership selection, ownership transfer, and estate planning. I'll discuss each of these thoroughly in the chapters ahead.

As you obtain information and make decisions—or if circumstances change—you'll have to revisit these areas, since they influence one another. For example, your designated successor may decide not to work in the family business after all, necessitating a return to the selection process. You'd also have to adjust your estate-planning documents to reflect the change and then set up a new strategy for conveying ownership to a different successor.

Like a cross-country trip, this three-part journey needs to be broad in scope and go beyond just appointing a new leader. You and all the other stakeholders must address many topics, set specific milestones, and write everything down.

2. What Is Your Timetable?

Once you become clear about the route you'll be taking, you must establish a detailed timetable to help move the journey along. This is often the longest part of succession planning. As with achieving desired results of any kind, though, *if you can't measure your progress, you can't control the process.*

When scheduling a road trip, you must allow for emergencies, like a flat tire or an accident. You must do the same when laying out your succession timeline. A crisis can come up and, presto, the gods have changed the game. For example, a major customer could suddenly switch to a competitor, a key family member in the business could die suddenly or divorce, or an environmental issue could pop up with a resulting lawsuit. These unforeseen events could drag out this scheduling step even more—another reason to start the journey as soon as possible.

3. Who Is the Navigator?

You will need to choose someone to take the lead not only in charting the course but also in making sure all participants adhere to it and the timetable. The current CEO typically assumes this role, though not always. In my case, my dad kept talking about what he would do regarding succession, but he took no action. I ultimately needed to step in and drive the process.

The navigator must possess strong people and listening skills, and demonstrate sensitivity to all family members. The ideal person, if not the outgoing leader or the successor, may be a relative within the organization or a consultant from the outside. Have a family meeting to vote for the best candidate.

The navigator needs to move the planning along but in a patient, empathetic way. Although most businesses must rigidly stay on schedule, in the natural ebb and flow of the transition, the timeline should be used as a benchmark.

One of the most frustrating challenges I faced during succession and estate planning was getting my father to accept my consultant choices, particularly concerning insurance and estate taxes. My dad would say, "I hate insurance salesmen." And that would be the end of the discussion for him.

He did agree to attend to an estate-planning seminar sponsored by a consulting firm that one of his contacts had recommended to him. We worked with one of their advisors who constructed a plan for us, but about five years later, we discovered that we had been overinsured and paying far too much.

> **As navigator in my transition, I had to be sensitive to my dad's strengths and limitations and stay especially alert to his difficulty in letting go of the business.**

The same thing happened with an industrial psychologist. Since I wanted someone my dad would feel comfortable with, I let him choose the counselor we would use. He got a name from one of his associates, but once again, he ended up hating the consultant. I agreed that I didn't want to work with the person anymore either.

As navigator in my transition, I had to be sensitive to my dad's strengths and limitations and stay especially alert to his difficulty in letting go of the business. I knew he liked to lead, so I always made him feel as though he were in charge. Consequently, he believed he was winning the battles, but I knew I was winning the war.

> Route + Timetable + Navigator = Successful Transition Journey

Commitment a Must

All family members who work or have a stake in the business must take part in planning and completing every stage of the transition journey. Even though people by nature don't like change or having to step out of their comfort zone, everyone needs to be accountable to the plan. Then, it will be in each person's interest to pay close attention and raise a red flag if things aren't progressing according to the agreed-upon guidelines. Here, the navigator can play an important role in helping resolve disputes between the various temperaments involved.

The number of relatives participating can certainly influence the degree of complexity of the decision-making process. Establishing consensus takes time—one *more* reason to start early. Since my father and I were the only family members working in the business, we didn't have to contend with bringing together multiple relatives to reach agreement. Even so, my father promoted me to president in 1997, but he didn't finally get out of the day-to-day running of the business until seven years later. It just always takes longer than expected to transfer leadership from one generation to the next.

Most importantly, the succession-planning process requires a commitment from the top down. A stress-free transition will not occur if leaders talk a good game about passing the baton but continue to express through their actions a deep resistance about ever letting go. This lack of dedication to the process spells disaster from the start.

At the same time, a successor must also make a commitment and accept with great confidence and enthusiasm the prospect of leading the company into the future. It is unwise to force family members to take on any position in the business, let alone the chief executive role, if they are feeling at all reluctant. This will only create more problems than solutions and bring about family discord down the road.

For example, a friend of mine whose father owned one of the world's largest and most successful ad agencies, knew his father was a control freak—as evidenced by the fact that the number two position at the agency was a revolving door. The old man was always firing people for not meeting up to his impossible standards ("Nobody can do it as well as I can"). The smartest thing my friend ever did was realize such an environment was not for him. He could not commit himself to the family business. Instead, he charted his own course in another industry and achieved great success. So it is possible that an effective succession process will, in fact, lead to a different path than was otherwise thought. Determining the level of commitment from the top down will help reveal that path.

Insider Tip #22

To increase the likelihood of a positive transition, the CEO, successor, and family stakeholders must fully dedicate themselves to the process and participate in all decision making.

Success Stories

So far, I've given you numerous examples of transitions or exit strategies that went horribly wrong due to a lack of or inefficient succession planning. Let me balance the score a bit by presenting two positive ones.

The first involves the Burlington Coat Factory, a New Jersey mom-and-pop store that eventually grew to thirty-two locations throughout the country. In 1983, with second-generation Monroe Milstein at the helm, the family business was doing so well that it went public. The company's growing success was due in no small part to its efficient, mostly family-run operation. Each person had a specific area of responsibility and respected the division of labor by never challenging one another's autonomy.

For example, Monroe's wife, Henny, ran the children's wear division, and their sons Steve and Andrew ran the menswear and women's sportswear divisions, respectively. Monroe's oldest son, Lazar, focused on the company's information technology group. In addition, a non–family member, Jerry Zelman, served as operations manager. When he died in 1982, just as the company was going public, another non–family member, Mark Nesci, replaced him.

The subject of transition planning didn't come up as such until the 1990s when the company's stock analyst asked Monroe (then in his sixties) if he had a succession plan. He responded, "I'll be chairman emeritus, and my youngest sons and Mark can run the company. They'll work it out between them."

In the end, the Milsteins wisely agreed to sell the business instead of sharing leadership responsibility. Had they chosen to keep the company, with Monroe staying on as chairman, they predicted that conflicts would have been inevitable. Eventually, the four of them would have begun forming alliances against one another as friction mounted over decisions they each made.

Because the Milsteins all loved the business, they confided in a close friend to help them process their decision to sell. This friend advised them to attend a YPO Family Business Seminar to aid them in ironing out the details of an exit strategy without acrimony. The program helped all of them, especially Steve, who still had reservations about walking away from the family business. He voted with his father and brother to sell, agreeing with them that it was easier, more practical, and better for the company's future to split the cash from the sale of the business rather than splitting the business itself.

This is how the transition journey should unfold, regardless of the ultimate business outcome.

For another example of a properly crafted and executed succession plan, we can turn to Modell's Sporting Goods. Founded in 1889, this is one of America's oldest family-owned sporting goods and apparel retailers. Mitchell and Michael Modell became the fourth-generation owners of the business when their father decided to step down after forty years. Because their father had always envisioned his boys taking over the business, he began laying the groundwork early on to ensure an easy transition. He bought out his daughter (the boys' sister) so they could start with a clean slate. No other family members would be involved in a decision-making capacity. He started estate planning as well.

Similar to the Burlington Coat Factory team, the Modell boys have well-defined roles and responsibilities as coleader. Although their father continued to have a presence in the business, he operated as if he weren't there. His philosophy with regard to his sons' leadership was to let the chips fall where they may. Having no problem with letting go of the reins, he said to his sons, "You'll either make it or break it." He managed to keep any of his concerns about their leadership at the door—always a key ingredient in a successful transition.

As their first action milestone after taking over, Mitchell and Michael set up a board of advisors from the retail industry. The brothers directed this board to continually ask them the tough questions and push them to achieve ever-greater degrees of professionalism and expertise in the business.

As their second action milestone, they hired an industrial psychologist to help them communicate and resolve any issues of control or disputes about decisions. If one brother has a disagreement with the other, rather than letting it fester into a wound that might damage their relationship, *together* they call the industrial psychologist for assistance. The coleaders' clear-cut roles also help speed up conflict resolution.

> If one brother has a disagreement with the other, rather than letting it fester into a wound that might damage their relationship, *together* they call the industrial psychologist for assistance.

Largely because of how much Mitchell and Michael trust and respect each other, the company has flourished under their direction. The proof is in the numbers: they took an already-profitable company doing $18 million in annual sales when their dad stepped down to doing more than $650 million (with no debt) today. The boys definitely have retail in their blood.

Insider Tip #23

An effective succession may involve selling the business or choosing dual leaders—explore all possibilities and be willing to brainstorm creative solutions.

The general who wins the battle makes many calculations in his temple before the battle is fought. The general who loses makes but few calculations beforehand.

—Sun Tzu

A Good Match
Choosing the Right Replacement

Paul was the only son of the owner of the family business. The apple of his dad's eye, he was the ideal blood heir to assume the throne of the impressive fragrance house that made essential oils for the cosmetics and health and beauty industries. He loved the business, the employees, and the customers, but his difficulties with his dad dominated the workplace.

Paul's dad was a headstrong, almost larger-than-life figure. Living up to his expectations during the transition period was no easy task for Paul, who quickly grew confused by his dad's mixed signals about who was in control—a confusion that quickly led to a power struggle between them.

The company had been quite successful, and by the time Paul took over in the early '80s, it was flush with cash. The election of the pro-business Ronald Reagan signaled that profits would continue to climb. Unfortunately, though, the growing lack of communication between Paul and his iron-willed dad made for such a rocky transition that Paul eventually turned to drugs to escape.

Cocaine was his narcotic of choice. It was expensive, but plentiful—and so was the money Paul had available to buy it. Before long, his drug habit, the conflicting messages from his dad, and the pain of their deteriorating relationship took a toll on both of them. The business suffered greatly as well, and ultimately they were forced to sell.

Who was to blame for this sad outcome? The short answer is no one—and everyone.

Paul's dad may not have been able to foresee that passing the baton to his only son would destroy everything he had put his life into, but he was at fault for never considering such a possibility. He failed to lay out an objective selection process that might have exposed some of his son's flaws and his own. He had allowed himself to be ruled entirely by emotion—first when choosing a successor ("he's my only son!") and then throughout the leadership changeover, which he had never fully committed to or he wouldn't have delivered all those mixed signals.

He failed to lay out an objective selection process that might have exposed some of his son's flaws and his own. He had allowed himself to be ruled entirely by emotion.

Completely overwhelmed at trying to get out from under the shadow of his old man and lacking the will or the temperament to stand up to him, Paul had thus sought escape from *everything* in drugs. He not only derailed his own succession but also brought about the implosion of the entire organization itself.

Blindly pinning all your hopes on one child to someday take over the family business can be fraught with peril. If you luck out and the stars perfectly align—the child has a head and a passion for the business and you are sincerely committed to letting go and giving your successor full control—you can expect a smooth transition. But if the solar system falls out of sync, as in the story of Paul and his dad, your business—everything you've worked so hard to build—will likely collapse.

Whether you have one child or multiple offspring, when you're choosing a successor, stay as emotionally detached as possible and commit to a methodical approach. In the case of Paul and his dad, everything from the selection process to the planning and management of the transition was left to chance. Do not let this happen to you.

Insider Tip #24

Don't kid yourself into thinking that the leadership transfer in a family business will magically work itself out because blood is thicker than water. You must take deliberate, impartial action to locate the best new leader.

Designing the Job First

In any organization with a human resources department, a job description is written before the interviewing process even begins. In a family business, the CEO, senior executives, and participating family members must follow the same practice when choosing a successor for the company leader—something Paul's dad should have done. Every business must establish titles and areas of responsibility for management positions, but this is particularly critical in a family-owned one. Lines can easily blur when disagreements between family members in those positions arise (and they most often will). It should always be clear from the person's title or area of responsibility who shall have the final say.

As current leader, you need to craft a thorough job description for your own replacement, whether you make successor decisions on your own or together with the senior leadership team. You must incorporate everything you have learned over the years running the business and assess how your strengths and weaknesses have contributed to creating the present business culture (for better or worse). For a family business, you must consider the vision you and the family have for its future and determine what the organization will need from its new leader to take it to the next level—for example, greater expertise in the financial arena, more sales acumen, superior skills at innovating, and better management skills. You must clarify those needs *before* any action is taken to look for a new CEO.

Addressing these topics will yield a clear picture of the exact kind of successor you are looking for. Of course, as with hiring anyone, you won't know if you've chosen well until you've afforded the replacement the opportunity to actually perform the work. But you can certainly increase your odds of success by including the following key qualities in your job description:

- **Passion.** How excited is the candidate at the prospect of accepting such a demanding position? Is the person driven with the sense of opportunity and full of questions and ideas? In my mind, passion is the most important quality to look for in a successor. I can't envision a company functioning smoothly and growing more profitable under someone without it. The leader needs to inspire employees to be more productive and customers to be more interested in partnering. Does the candidate exhibit the kind of sincere fervor most likely to energize people?

- **Proficiency.** What type of education, training, and outside experience does the candidate have? If the person has strong financial skills (and that's the strength you are looking for), but lacks sales or technical savvy, can you train the person in these areas?

- **People skills.** Is the candidate a people person? Leonard Lauder, chairman emeritus of the Estée Lauder Companies, believes that the CEO's role is to "lead passionately with compassion." That comment has always resonated with me. To be an accomplished leader, you need to understand and empathize with people so they will come to actually *share* your passion, not just be steamrolled by it into doing what you want.

- **Perseverance.** Will the candidate remain calm in crisis? How does he or she process the inevitable chaos of today's business world? Whether dealing with customers, associates, a difficult business climate, or just day-to-day concerns, a CEO must be determined to achieve success. Life is full of inconsistencies and ups and downs; a good candidate should embody a take-no-prisoners attitude, never giving up and always keeping the company's goals in sight.

On the flip side, you need to avoid some behaviors at all costs. Here are the most troubling ones:

- **Introversion.** All leaders aren't backslapping extroverted types, nor should they be. But those who stay in their office all the time behind closed (and locked) doors aren't leaders—they're hiding. A potential successor with a reputation for choosing solitude over engagement will cripple communication throughout the organization and generate a widespread feeling of "every man for himself!" And customers accustomed to an accessible leader will feel similarly isolated, grow frustrated, and likely go elsewhere.

- **Explosive temperament.** There is no question about it: Most employees will jump ship quickly if they have a screamer for a boss. No one wants to be yelled at all the time or subjected to other abusive treatment from an angry, unstable individual of any kind—let alone an employer. That sort of disposition in a leader virtually guarantees a constantly (and costly) revolving door.

- **Lack of integrity.** Deceptive CEOs who don't keep their word set a bad example. This unprofessional way of operating telegraphs a host of contradictory messages— paramount of which is making promises with little or no intention of keeping them. Such behavior often reveals an absence of honesty and principles, something that employees—and customers—can smell a mile off. So make sure your nose is working.

- **Negativism.** Those who always see the glass as half-empty are like energy vampires: They drain everyone's strength and spirit. As I mentioned in chapter 3, people like this can be toxic to an organization. As leaders, they can spread the negativism disease from the top down, sapping initiative and innovation.

    Public criticism works the same way. In wine baron Robert Mondavi's autobiography, *Harvests of Joy: How the Good Life Became Great Business*, (Harcourt, 1998), the author expressed regret at his tendency to publicly disparage his employees, a significant factor in the loss of his own two sons as allies in the business. Mondavi acknowledged belatedly that he should have saved any criticism for private moments.

    Enough negativity permeates the business world as it is without adding more by choosing a nay-saying, belittling successor.

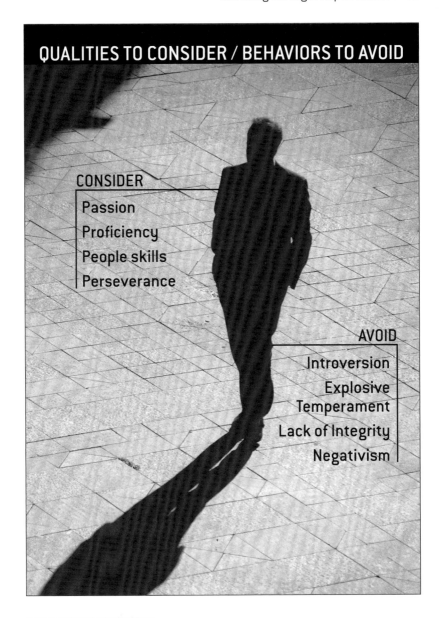

QUALITIES TO CONSIDER / BEHAVIORS TO AVOID

CONSIDER
Passion
Proficiency
People skills
Perseverance

AVOID
Introversion
Explosive Temperament
Lack of Integrity
Negativism

Insider Tip #25

Look for passion as the top quality in your replacement. Your company's future depends on having a leader who can excite and motivate people.

Looking for the Best Fit

When choosing a new leader for a family business, you can search for candidates in three places:

1. Within the family

2. Outside the family but within the business

3. Outside the family *and* the business: a hired gun

A number of factors can complicate the search for someone within the family: the makeup of the family itself (number of relatives in the business), family politics, and the capabilities and temperaments of the individuals involved (who should be considered and who should be avoided like the plague). This last challenge is not confined to just a family business, however. All organizations must take the same painstaking steps in evaluating applicants to find the right leader.

In my case, this search was made easier because my father had only one son and one daughter and he envisioned early on that I would be the one to eventually take over the business. That was not because he favored his only son, but because, as I noted earlier in this book's introduction, Viviane's interests lay elsewhere in linguistics and video production, not in packaging and printing. Fortunately, I demonstrated both a passion and an aptitude for leading Arkay, thus preserving our family legacy.

In other families, however, intense feuding can occur around selecting a new CEO, and only an outsider with a proven track record will pass muster with everyone as the best choice. To keep the business intact, they may be forced to pass it on to a non-family member. But no matter where the successor comes from, a strategic plan must then be established for the grooming process—a plan that fully aligns with the company's vision and expectations.

Grooming a New Leader

The process of preparing a leader for succession should begin as soon as the leader is chosen. Once that happens, the current CEO needs to assume a mentoring role and implement a flexible yet formal program of sharing company history, work experience, and insights into the business and its customers.

When several strong candidates are being considered for the leadership position, I suggest an initial tryout period to determine which one will undergo the grooming process. For example, let's say that two brothers and a sister are vying for the job. Allow one sibling to run sales, one to run finances, and the third to run the marketing department for a period in keeping with the timeline for transition. They should have all the responsibility and accountability connected with their jobs, including being reviewed regularly and evaluated as toughly (but not more so) on their performance as any other employee. Budgets, forecasts, and so on, should all be laid out for them as well.

> Standard sibling rivalries and friction may exist at first, but out of the turmoil, natural leadership and dominance skills will surface, and the best candidate will rise above the rest.

The CEO and senior management can see how the candidates handle pressure and respond to the various crises—typical and otherwise—that come up in the everyday running of the business. Standard sibling rivalries and friction may exist at first, but out of the turmoil, natural leadership and dominance skills will surface, and the best candidate will rise above the rest. Who knows—dual leaders may even emerge.

After this trial run, the winning candidate (or candidates) must then be given decision-making responsibilities immediately to demonstrate successor worthiness. The incumbent leader, with the help of the management team, needs to establish some specific objectives in various areas that the candidates must research and determine how to accomplish. Results should be measurable— the only true way of gauging anyone's job performance, especially that of a CEO. Easy at first, these assignments should grow increasingly more complex to evaluate the new leader's progress.

In addition to such obvious tasks as lowering inventory and payroll expenses, and narrowing the divide (days outstanding) between accounts receivable and sales, here are five measurable actions relevant to all businesses that you can use to evaluate the successor-in-training's skills and competence:

1. **Reduce debt.** This involves cutting the amount of principal and interest payments made to banks and other institutions for loans, notes, bonds, mortgages, or any other form of debt obligation.

2. **Improve efficiencies.** As an example, in the printing business, we define the term "make-ready" as the period between the end of one job and the beginning of another. As an incoming leader, I had to have a firm grip on the various factors that determined the length of this interval (factory conditions, crew capabilities, and so on) in order to boost productivity.

3. **Grow year-over-year sales.** A rise in the percentage of earnings from sales from one year to the next that you can attribute to the new leader's efforts provides a clear gauge of the positive direction his or her direction would take the company. This performance should be evaluated over an eighteen- to twenty-four-month period.

4. **Increase EBITDA.** Otherwise referred to as earnings before interest, taxes, depreciation, and amortization, this mea-

surement refers to the amount of cash flow a company has for operations. Its relative size at the end of the targeted period demonstrates the successor CEO's ability to improve the business's cash flow and enterprise value.

5. **Strengthen the balance sheet.** The candidate must show skills in managing the company's balance sheet. By understanding the value of the business at a specific point in time, leaders can better measure its financial health.

Because candidates must exercise their own judgment in handling these tasks, they must be given the chance to make mistakes. Instead of stepping in and fixing things, the outgoing leader needs to take a more Socratic stance and ask the candidate questions without providing the answers. The best gift my dad gave me, once the succession roles were defined, was allowing me to make difficult decisions in my new job. He would share his thoughts, of course, but ultimately I had to rely on my own thinking—and my decision was final.

> The world won't come crashing down if you give the incoming leader room to fail on occasion. The most important lessons I learned as a new CEO came from making mistakes.

The world won't come crashing down if you give the incoming leader room to fail on occasion. The most important lessons I learned as a new CEO came from making mistakes. Although painful, my blunders turned me into a stronger, more resourceful business owner and manager. Any errors made at this time should be viewed as opportunities for growth and improvement.

A final decision regarding the new leader's competency can often be made within twenty-four to thirty-six months after the grooming begins. At that time, the outgoing leader, along with other senior managers if they are part of the process, should be able to clearly assess the candidate's ability to assume control of the family business.

The more the incumbent is willing to stand back during this two- to three-year period, the more confidence the successor will gain and the more faith the former will have in the latter (and in the process). This, in turn, gives rise to a faster, more peaceful changeover and a win-win for everybody involved—including the company and the rest of the family.

Many businesses can't (or choose not to) afford themselves the luxury of engaging in such a practice. The leader may die prematurely without a succession plan in place or resist the transition, inwardly hoping it will fall apart and force the family or board members to turn to him to rescue the business from the brink. No one should underestimate the ego's extremely powerful influence at times like these. Outgoing CEOs must *fully embrace* the role of mentor, focusing on what works and filtering out what doesn't. Incoming ones should do the same with the role of successor. It works both ways.

Insider Tip #26

To set the stage for future success, the current leadership must give a successor-in-training the freedom to make mistakes. So often, CEOs stall the transition process because they're afraid to see their replacement fail.

Creating Harmony

Someone once said to me, "I will know I've been a success as a father if my children want to hang out with me when they get older." Succession plans are like that too. If they are put together and managed in a thoughtful, respectful, and nurturing manner, outgoing leaders will be heroes. Incoming leaders will feel empowered, having overcome the grooming period's many hurdles, and will appreciate all the help their predecessors gave along the way—and will therefore always consider them a source of sage counsel. Family members will still be speaking to one another, and the businesses will remain intact.

Clearly, selecting the right successor can be a challenge. The lives of everyone who works for or has a stake in the company, including its customers, and the fate of the company itself lie in the balance. The best way to meet such a challenge is with a sound succession plan and execution process that all parties can trust and take part in.

Employees will grow more confident and secure in the future as they witness that future unfold under the tested leadership of the incoming successor. In the same way, suppliers, customers—and even family members—will respond favorably to the changes to come if they perceive the positive results. As always, the more you give as a leader, the more likely your business and your family will coexist in harmony.

Insider Tip #27

Upon succession, set a plan to deliver immediate and measurable results to one area of the business. A quick success will build confidence in the new leader, the new team—and the organization.

Before you can really start setting financial goals,
you need to determine where you stand financially.

—David Bach

EIGHT

He Who Has the Gold

Transferring Ownership

Max Kaneff, my grandfather, groomed my dad to lead Arkay, making him president when Howard turned twentynine. Yet upon Max's death, my dad's mother received half the company shares, and Howard had to split the other half with his sister, Florence. Although he officially presided over Arkay's operations, my dad's minority interest in the family business severely limited his power.

The situation worsened after my grandmother passed away. Howard discovered that shortly before their mother's death from Alzheimer's, my aunt Florence had manipulated her into changing her will. As a result, my dad found himself completely cut from his mother's estate. He had to buy out 50 percent of his sister's interest in the family business, which had been intended for him. Naturally, my dad viewed Florence's act as a betrayal, leading him to stop speaking to her for fifteen years.

As this unfortunate chapter in our family history illustrates, a successor's ability to lead hinges on his or her degree of control over the family business. As my dad experienced himself, for an effective transition, the new CEO must have access to ownership for the obvious reason that whoever has the most shares in the company pulls the most strings. To that end, this part of the succession journey focuses on determining the status of the ownership and control in the company and on developing a plan to convey a majority of the shares to the new leader.

Who Owns What?

Typically, family members own a certain percentage of equity in the business in the form of voting or nonvoting shares. As part of ownership-transfer planning, CEOs, their designated successor, and other shareholders must explore and answer two questions: (1) who holds majority interest? and (2) where is the company headed? Let's take them in order:

1. Who Holds Majority Interest?

Depending on the size of the business, the shareholder landscape can be quite complex. To sort out ownership and fully understand its ramifications, review where your company stands in the following areas:

- How large is the family? (that is, are there multiple siblings, stepparents, aunts, and uncles with controlling interests?)

- How are the company shares divided? Who is the majority shareholder?

- How many of the shareholders are willing to convey their shares to the next-generation leader? How will shares be transferred? Will the outgoing leader gift shares, or will the successor have an opportunity to buy them over time?

- If the incumbent is the majority shareholder and quite elderly, how will estate taxes be paid if he dies unexpectedly before ownership is transferred? Nothing can beat Uncle Sam in devouring the assets of a business if an estate plan is not in place to cover the possibility of excessive taxation.

If all involved parties agree to transfer shares, they need to lay out a strategy for making that happen. In my case, my dad learned from his father's mistakes and gifted me Arkay shares throughout my childhood. How-ard used business downturns—and thus lowered valuations—as oppor-tunities to pass on a greater part of the company to me. Although oth-erwise undesirable, such times do provide family businesses the means to hasten the ownership transfer while reducing gift and estate taxes.

If the majority shares cannot be conveyed to the heir apparent for some reason, he or she will have to decide whether that's acceptable.

If, however, the majority shares cannot be conveyed to the heir apparent for some reason, he or she will have to decide whether that's acceptable. CEOs, in keeping with their mentor-ing role, can help with this decision-making process by encourag-ing successors to ask themselves these personal questions:

- Can I handle *not* being the sole or majority owner?

- Can I deal with sharing ownership and leadership re-sponsibility with other family members?

- Do I have respect for, and is there mutual respect among, all the family members with whom I may have to share responsibility?

- If not, do I think I can overcome it?

2. Where Is the Company Headed?

Some family businesses exist solely as a vehicle for creating a comfortable lifestyle (travel, cars, vacations, and so forth) for the family. Working relatives receive a salary, own some percentage of stock in the company, and make a little money year after year in ownership equity, paying the lowest taxes possible. Happy with this arrangement, they want it to continue into the future.

In effect, this is the company's mission statement: status quo forever.

Other businesses have a philosophy of "pump and dump." This established tactic calls for capturing more market share in the company's respective product line(s) with the goal of selling out at the best time to a strategic investor, equity investor, or employee stock ownership plan (ESOP).

Of course, without a crystal ball, no one can predict exactly where an organization will be in five to ten years. But for good indicators of its future standing, I recommend looking at sign-posts such as the company's current position in the marketplace, the nature of the competition, and the strength and loyalty of the customer base.

Asking these "fork in the road" questions will expose every-one's thinking. It also provides the opportunity to discuss the plan for the business, if one exists, and to determine the degree to which all family members are committed to it. Participants need to talk about what it entails to grow, sell, or pass the baton, along with the consequences of taking no action. This leg of the suc-cession journey can help everyone clarify goals and expectations, prompting further conversations about family values and tradi-tions and about whether the business plan needs to change—or be created—to align with them.

During this process, designated successors may decide to turn down the leadership position. Upon learning they will have to share ownership with other family members, they may opt out of assuming a lesser role. Or perhaps their vision for the business runs contrary to the current mission slated to remain under their command. They may want to hold on to the company and make it even more of an industry force, instead of building it just to sell. Rather than subject themselves to the conflicts arising from incompatible goals, they may prefer to work elsewhere.

Alternatively, these discussions may uncover several areas of agreement. Everyone—or a majority of participants—may welcome the successor's plans to sustain and grow the business, thereby unifying family members and solidifying the new leader's resolve to assume control.

Insider Tip #28

Take advantage of recessions and other low-income periods to transfer more value to the heir apparent and reduce tax consequences.

Financial Stewardship

To convey ownership shares to your successor, you will need to determine the fair-market valuation of your business. Among other requirements, this process calls for following smart accounting procedures and closely monitoring your company's condition.

As a matter of course, you should adopt these best practices to sustain and build your organization. In fact, as you transfer ownership to the heir apparent, I recommend transferring a culture of financial stewardship as well—not only to preserve your family's legacy but also to facilitate the leadership changeover. Your efforts in this area will greatly improve your successor's ability to meet immediate and long-term goals.

Most families have a few skeletons in the closet, and in a family-held business, one or two may be lurking deep in the books as well. Although accounting irregularities can result innocently enough from poor record keeping, they can also arise from a fraudulent attempt to increase profits in order to obtain lenders or investors.

> **Most families have a few skeletons in the closet, and in a family-held business, one or two may be lurking deep in the books as well.**

As I explained in chapter 2, a former CFO at Arkay hid information from me when I first took over the company. He purposely overstated our assets and manipulated expenses by not writing off uncollectible accounts receivable, obsolete inventory, and outdated equipment and by improperly capitalizing items that should have been expensed. He inflated the company's value in assets, allowing the balance sheet to look stronger, and in turn inflated profits.

Today, I work closely with our CFO, Darlene Triglia, to make sure that we are clearly accountable for all our financial reports. I now sign all checks and review our weekly deposit checks. She and I believe strongly in upholding the integrity and accuracy of Arkay's financials. This commitment gives us great peace of mind when we plan the short- and long-term goals for the company.

Regular Fiscal Checkups

Successful leaders constantly evaluate their business performance. They examine historical data, competitor achievements, and unrelated organizations that have proved successful. Of course, they also look at sales, profits, and total assets. Chief executives must be able to read between the lines of financial statements to fully assess their company's well-being.

For me, this evaluation process is analogous to what occurs during a routine medical checkup. When I go for my physical, the doctor performs several tests and carefully reviews the results. Some of those tests provide snapshots of my health (a chest x-ray or red blood count), while others provide information over time (an EKG). In a similar way, leaders must conduct a regular exam of their business—and pass the practice on to their successor. This checkup includes analyzing the three major financial reports: the cash flow statement, the balance sheet, and the income statement. Like medical tests, these reports will give you either a snapshot of your organization's condition (the balance sheet) or information over time (the cash flow and income statements).

Insider Tip #29

At the start of the transition, the outgoing and incoming leaders must work together as internists in evaluating the company's financial health.

The Cash Flow Statement

Begin a fiscal checkup by evaluating cash flow activities for a particular accounting period. This information is typically divided into three categories on a financial statement: operating (payroll and cash receipts and payments), investing (capital expenditures and investment proceeds), and financing (debt payments and loan proceeds).

As you study the data, you might discover that a negative cash flow is looming because family members are sucking too much money out of the business. Since this could threaten future growth and profitability, you will obviously need to make adjustments. Or in reviewing how the company plans to meet cash demands, you might uncover covenants with various banks or lenders that charge penalties when excess cash is withdrawn.

It is, therefore, imperative to also estimate future cash flow needs. Your appraisal must take into account any projected salaries, bonuses, other operating expenses, investments, and debt. This will help you manage your discretionary and nondiscretionary expenditures (such as gifting your children $12,000 worth of company shares only to discover you could have given more—a substantial oversight if left uncorrected).

The Balance Sheet

A summary of assets, liabilities, and shareholders' equity, the balance sheet provides a picture of your company's fitness on a specific date. My father instilled in me the habit of watching Arkay's financial trends, so I recommend analyzing this information over three-year intervals. Here are the key metrics I review:

1. **Debt-to-Equity Ratio.** To meet their growth plans, leaders must understand how much money they can borrow over time. A highly leveraged balance sheet could jeopardize the business long term, an important consideration if the strategy is to sell, refinance, or purchase another company. Too much debt can also undermine the valuation of the company, resulting in less-favorable business terms. Generally, I like to keep the debt-to-equity ratio well below 40 percent to avoid liquidity problems.

2. **Asset-to-Liability Ratio.** Considered a test of liquidity of a company, the asset-to-liability ratio can help CEOs determine whether their growth plan is leading to wealth or debt. Usually, it is a good practice to maintain a 2:1 ratio between assets and liabilities. Overall, though, remember that debt is not a four-letter word. To fuel expansion, acquiring debt is oftentimes a necessary strategy. Many companies—for example, Howard Johnson Hotels Inc.—failed to grow because, although remaining debt free, they refused to adequately invest in their product to meet the changing needs of the marketplace.

3. **Inventory Levels.** Health signs pertaining to cash flow will vary with the type of business—service, manufacturing, or financial—and industry. Nevertheless, you need to constantly look for ways to free up cash within your organization.

As a manufacturer, I regularly investigate inventory levels and ask the following questions:

- Is it possible to manufacture or produce just-in-time products?

- Can we purchase raw materials on consignment and pay for them as they're used?

- How can I shorten the manufacturing or selling cycle?

I reduced inventory levels at Arkay by analyzing finished goods with my team. We discovered we were producing 10 to 15 percent above the needed quantities. Historically, many of these items would sell, but in the last decade, I found that we were actually internally destroying large quantities of inventory we overproduced. By cutting back on production, we freed up our machines to manufacture other sellable products. Our cash flow then increased because we weren't purchasing as much material, and our profitability rose because we weren't writing off huge obsolete inventories.

The Income Statement

The income statement provides a summary of your company's performance over a specific accounting period, usually a fiscal quarter or year. It reports revenue and expenses for both operating and nonoperating activities, as well as the net profit or loss incurred.

As I pointed out in chapter 1, Eliyahu Goldratt emphasizes in his book *The Goal* that we are in business primarily to make money. So to be financially fit over the longer term, I suggest examining your income statement for trends in expenses, operating profitability, retained earnings of the organization, and EBITDA (earnings before interest, taxes, depreciation, and amortization). This analysis will help you pinpoint what you need to do to make your company more profitable. Also, when reviewing these numbers, I always look to see how we compare with the competition and general industry benchmarks.

*

All family members involved in the business, either in the day-to-day operations, on the board, or as shareholders, should take part in these regular fiscal checkups to gain consensus and build commitment to the future. I recommend that participants draw up a family employment and compensation policy to clearly define salaries, bonuses, and distributions, thereby reducing resentment and confusion. Family members should also discuss methods for conserving capital in the organization.

With such proper planning and smart business practices, cash needs can be carefully monitored, ensuring that the financial part of the transition between generations is seamless.

Insider Tip #30

Use external auditors to objectively review your company's financials since they can recognize potential problems and present workable solutions to improve your bottom line.

Estate planning is people: spouses, children, grandchildren, favorite family members, and close friends. It is state and federal taxes: income, death, gift. It is lawyers, accountants, insurance people, banks, and financial planners. It is a world of advisors busily accomplishing things that most people do not understand.

—**Robert A. Esperti and Renno L. Peterson,**
Protect Your Estate

NINE

After the Funeral
Preparing for the Unknown

J. R. is the president and co-owner of a closely held production company that has been family run for more than a century. He took over when his dad, who was then inactive in the business but held 70 percent of the common voting stock, died unexpectedly. When originally drawn up, his father's will left all assets to his surviving spouse. An added predecease clause stated, though, that if his wife predeceased him, the assets would go to their three children: J. R. and his two sisters (one older and one younger), neither of whom worked in the family business. Moreover, the clause drilled down to the next of kin should all three siblings expire. So far, so good.

But now . . . the nightmare!

J. R. had not stuck his nose into reviewing and updating his father's will because, frankly, he had always assumed that his dad was attending to it. How wrong he was! J. R.'s father had not looked at his will for at least a decade before his death. And during the intervening years, his wife (J. R.'s mom) had passed on. But the attorney who had assisted in administering her will and codicil never advised her husband to update his own will after she was gone to reflect this and other changes—such as the fact that their eldest daughter, who had three children from two different marriages, had also died during the same intervening period. This meant that in order to buy the business outright and run it himself, J. R. would have to negotiate an agreement not only with his still-living younger sister but also with his late elder sister's three offspring!

To compound these mounting succession and ownership headaches, the valuation of his late father's majority share gave rise to an estate tax that could lead to severe liquidity problems. J. R. and the other survivors were worried that they'd have to sell off the business to an outsider to cover this debt.

His lack of foresight ultimately jeopardized a family-income staple and business legacy that had existed in the community for more than one hundred years.

His father's negligence in putting a business plan in place—and involving J. R. and professional advisors in continually reviewing and updating that plan—proved ruinous. His lack of foresight ultimately jeopardized a family-income staple and business legacy that had existed in the community for more than one hundred years.

Protect Against Tragedy

No one likes talking about death. Nevertheless, family business owners or majority stockholders have a responsibility to ensure a smooth and orderly continuation of their company should any of them die unexpectedly, as happened in J. R.'s family. As leader, you must develop a plan and draw up documents that will carry out your wishes for the business you have spent years building.

If you have only just begun succession planning, it is imperative that you make this the first leg of your journey and put in place an emergency leadership plan at once. To do this, you must select someone who can run the company *right now*. This individual must be able to immediately step up to the plate as the company's new leader after you're gone and talk to customers, employees, and vendors in order to maintain stability and limit fear and chaos. You may choose to allow your board of advisors to participate in this major decision, at least in the short term. In addition to finding the right successor, they can also research alternative opportunities, such as selling the business.

As you proceed on your succession journey, you will eventually resolve whether the person you named as your successor is capable of leading or will serve better as just the face of the business to the outside world. If you discover that no family member or key manager can—or wants to—run the business after your passing, your best option may be to sell. You or your board must communicate this message to the business community, vendors, and employees affected by your decision, laying out plans for what will happen after the sale. Taking these steps benefits the surviving relatives, protecting them from having to deal with such challenging issues during a confusing, emotional time.

As J. R.'s story illustrates, tragic life events can drastically alter family-owned companies. I strongly urge business leaders and their families to fully educate themselves on the importance of estate and succession planning and to seek the help of experienced professionals.

Design an Estate-Planning Team

As the saying goes, the only two guarantees in life are death and taxes. The latter is affected by the former. Bad or nonexistent estate planning can trigger more and larger taxes at death. Although a major concern, taxes are certainly not the only variable. Fiduciary control of assets is (or should be). Every business owner, leader, or majority shareholder needs to develop an airtight succession plan that cannot be undermined by outside forces such as greedy kin or the vagaries of Murphy's Law: if anything can go wrong, it will go wrong—and usually at the worst possible time. Well, there is no worse possible time than at death.

One of my trusted business advisors, Bart Krupnick, CPA, has again and again seen family members change color like chameleons when confronted with the prospect of sharing a late relative's assets. Without legal documents (will, trusts, life insurance, and buy-sell agreements) clearly laying out the disposition of assets in a business transition, family members will argue over the decedent's intent with the executor, who must then attempt to interpret the law. These battles often turn into court cases that last for years, siphoning off the business assets and emptying the family coffers. The emotional wounds from this kind of turmoil can take generations to heal.

Family members change color like chameleons when confronted with the prospect of sharing a late relative's assets.

To prevent such sabotage and avoid other pitfalls, shrewd business leaders should assemble a coterie of trustworthy professional advisors. Depending upon the size and scope of the family business and its resources, your dream team should consist of one or more of the following competent consultants:

1. **Certified public accountant (CPA).** Accountants are often the team members most familiar with the leader's (and the company's) financial condition, income, and spending habits because of the bookkeeping and tax services they have provided over the years. A CPA qualified to value the business can make an important addition to the estate-

planning group when real estate and equipment appraisals may be required upon the death of the leader. I would recommend, however, also hiring a specialist whose sole purpose is business valuations.

2. **Attorney.** Since estate planning by definition means determining the legal distribution of assets to one's heirs, it is important to have a lawyer on the team (and probably more than one) who specializes in this sometimes highly complex area. To avoid minefields, you need someone not only who can draft all the necessary legal documents  to make your estate and succession objectives clear and their execution sound but who can also identify and help mitigate all the estate- and gift-tax ramifications.

3. **Insurance agent.** Insurance helps meet the financial needs of an estate plan so that the business can continue—needs such as debt repayment, probate fees, estate administration expenses, and taxes. With such liquidity available, family members won't be forced to dip into the estate or sell off the business to cover these costs. Typically, life insurance provides the necessary funds. Again, you will need a competent professional with more than just an awareness of this all-important aspect of estate planning.

4. **Money advisors.** No, the tellers at your local bank won't do. Your trusted group must encompass experts in financial planning and asset management. To meet the needs of both

the leader and the business, each consultant must excel at investing, risk management, and retirement planning.

> **Insider Tip #31**
>
> An estate-planning dream team can ensure that all pertinent documents are properly drafted, accurately signed, and safely stored in an accessible place ready for delivery at the right time.

Spell Out Intent

Once you have assembled your trusted team, begin developing an estate plan by analyzing the effect of taking no action. Ask yourself if any of your succession objectives would be carried out if you did absolutely nothing. Typically, the answer is no. So to safeguard your legacy, start an effective estate-planning process by gathering data and drawing up legal documents, the most basic of which are a will and a living trust.

Last Will and Testament

Extremely critical, a *will* contains your instructions for carrying out burial wishes, disposing of property, appointing a guardian for minor children, designating a personal representative to administer the estate (executor), and handling other personal and business affairs after your death. It spells out in detail how you'd like your assets distributed (excluding individual retirement accounts, jointly titled property, and beneficiary assets, like your 401(k), profit-sharing or pension plans, and any life insurance owned by you, your business, or your spouse), and explains your intent regarding ownership or leadership of the business.

This document will prevent your estate- and succession-planning goals from being overturned—because if you die without a will, the state will dictate who is entitled to your assets and perhaps even those of the business. But you must remember to update your will to accommodate any life changes, or it may not reflect your wishes at the time of your death. Nothing counts other than what is written in the will.

Let's say that you have a bad marriage and intend to end it, but you die without a will—or without changing your existing one—before initiating divorce proceedings. Chances are, your spouse from hell will be the beneficiary of your procrastinating ways. This turn of events will obviously do little to warm the heart of your chosen heir or that of your handpicked successor. Nor will it ensure that your estate plan objectives are met. But it will very likely cause you to roll over and over in your grave.

A Living Trust

Ideally, an estate plan will help you maintain control of your property even after you die—but also remove that property from the estate for tax purposes. To some degree, you can do this with a carefully drafted *living trust* document. Often coming with additional costs, trusts are available in a wide variety for different purposes, including trusts for making gifts to minors, trusts for making gifts to charities (charitable trusts), marital trusts, credit by-pass shelter trusts, life insurance trusts, grantor-retained annuity trusts, and so on.

Generally, establishing and maintaining a trust also means complying with one or more federal tax requirements, such as filing annual trust or gift tax returns, when the trusts are funded with your property. Note that a revocable trust offers no protection from estate taxes since all the assets held in such an entity come back into the estate for tax purposes upon death.

Keep 'Em Safe but Findable

Once you have completed your analysis, gathered all your data, and drawn up all the relevant documents needed to execute your estate-planning wishes, you need to store those documents in a bank deposit box, a personal safe, or other secure location where strangers or noninvolved parties cannot access them.

You need to let those close to you know where to find the documents. Inform family members or the trusted people you want to participate in administering your estate, such as a personal representative. In addition, you must direct them to call your attorney (remember to provide his or her contact information) upon your death to begin carrying out the instructions set forth in your plan. This will ensure that your estate is handled properly with oversight by your representative, legal professionals, and the courts. An open succession-planning process includes holding family meetings to discuss all these matters ahead of time.

Insider Tip #32

Spend the time and money to draw up estate-planning documents and keep them safe. It's a small price to pay for the security of knowing that no one will be able to claim more from your estate than you have entitled them to.

Update Your Plan Annually

Once you have created an estate plan with the help of your advisors, it is not enough to just sit back and relax, and pat yourself on the back for a job well done. Yes, you have done an excellent job. But you are not finished, not by a long shot.

You must routinely revisit your will and estate plans to make adjustments. State and federal tax legislation can change, along with the economy, family relationships, your personal life (remember what I wrote earlier about divorce), your goals, your health, and even the location of your principal residence. By periodically reviewing and updating your will and other documents, you will make sure that their terms continue to conform to your current thinking and estate- and succession-planning objectives.

Let me be more specific about the words "periodically reviewing." Given the fact that time stands still for no one and tends to move faster the older we get, it makes sense to examine plan documents and evaluate your circumstances *on an annual basis.*

For example, let's say your plan names a certain relative as the next CEO. As I suggested in chapter 8, it may be wise to employ a gifting approach that accelerates the ownership transfer during company downturns. If you don't assess your plan at least annually, you may miss such opportunities to take advantage of economic cycles.

Insider Tip #33

As the owner-leader of a family business, you should follow a well-planned, long-term gifting strategy that gives everything to your heirs during your lifetime—so that you ultimately die with nothing.

The willingness to change is a strength.

—**Jack Welch**

TEN

The Baton Handoff
Stepping Aside

Vinnie, the CEO of a successful tire distributorship in New Jersey, realized his best days were behind him and began thinking succession. He wisely transferred majority ownership of the company to his management team and set up an employee stock ownership plan (ESOP) for the other workers. This strategy helped bolster the pension system and increased the financial strength of the overall organization.

So far, so good.

But Vinnie just couldn't let go of his "baby." Despite deteriorating health, he refused to accept that he no longer had exclusive control of the organization he had fathered. Like many entrepreneurs who build a successful business from the ground up, he had devoted more of his life to raising his business than to raising his children and watching them grow. And now that the time had come for him to set it free, he was experiencing the same doubts and anxieties that many parents experience at this stage with their offspring.

Despite owning just a fraction of the business at this point, Vinnie continued to act as though he still owned 100 percent. He ignored the very succession plan he himself had put in place, refusing to allow his troops to take full command and lead the organization to the next level on their own. Time and again, his managers sought to implement different marketing, manufacturing, and growth strategies, but their efforts were repeatedly thwarted by Vinnie's stubborn resistance and veto pen.

"How long will he go on like this?" they kept asking one another—until they finally got so disgruntled by his controlling behavior and his denial of all the havoc it was causing that they resigned.

> Despite owning just a fraction of the business at this point, Vinnie continued to act as though he still owned 100 percent. He ignored the very succession plan he himself had put in place.

With that, the company's inevitable slide began. In time, it was sold off—all because Vinnie had, in the end, put himself first instead of the company and everything it represented. Selfishly, he had assumed the attitude "I'll step down when I'm good and ready." Bitterly ironic, the very determination to hang on that had helped him successfully launch and build the tire distributorship turned out to be what ultimately caused its demise.

Insider Tip #34

Letting go is a critical part of a successful transition. In fact, from the moment you take over a business, you must begin emotionally preparing for the day you relinquish power—otherwise, chaos will likely ensue.

Loss of Identity

When passing the baton during a track race, runners need to access all their training, skills, and techniques to ensure a smooth handoff. The baton carrier must know when to release the baton and the receiver must know when to take it. Both must be working together and running at the same speed to avoid dropping it and losing the race.

The same scenario applies to a leadership transfer in the business world. Some CEOs, though, fail to recognize that by passing the baton, they are simply finishing another leg in their company's ongoing relay race. With their self-worth and identity so wrapped up in their role as leader, they suffer a great loss when they let go. They feel as though they are surrendering to old age and an unwanted fate rather than taking part in a necessary and inevitable milestone event. And that can be overwhelming. After all, the unknown ("what's next for me?") can be a scary place—doubly scary if you're heading into it feeling like a castoff.

This is why I have stressed that CEOs need to be encouraged to adopt a mentorship role during the transition instead of being exiled from it. In a relay race, the best runners allow the baton and the receiver to synchronize their speeds. Likewise, the most successful outgoing and incoming leaders use the entire changeover period to allow the former to fully groom the latter. If departing leaders participate in this way, they will have peace of mind knowing the next generation can continue to carry the family baton. Their fear of stepping down will become less all-consuming, making them more apt to cheer on their replacement, just as relay runners do once they release the baton.

For my dad, giving up control happened in stages over several years, during which he proved to be both a mentor to me and a roadblock to my transition journey. I saw the first signs of his letting go after I proved to have the chops to lead Arkay into the future. I accomplished this by quickly learning as much as possible, an especially tough challenge for a dyslexic like me. I felt pressure to correctly answer every question he asked, as if I were taking a pop quiz in school. Whether he asked about a sales strategy or a printing-press problem, I had to respond with knowledge and perspective. After passing these tests again and again, I demonstrated to him that I was serious about my transition into the leadership role at Arkay. Stage 1 was complete—although in his mind, Dad was still in control.

Next, he let go a bit more after understanding our particular similarities and differences. Our management styles, for example, could not have been further apart. More analytical and methodical, he would take time to make a decision, with little input from his team. On the other hand, he saw that I trusted people and my intuition and that I made decisions after candid discussions with managers. Though at first he overturned many of our decisions, in time he began to trust us. Both employees and customers saw my potential. They, too, were convinced I could do the job. Dad took notice. Stage 2 was complete.

Still, he would not step aside entirely. Our team spent far too much time cleaning up the damage he had done by reversing or ignoring major decisions. As you learned in chapter 4, his behavior prompted me to assert myself and take full control by writing a formal letter stating that it was time for him to pass the baton and that "all great kings retire." My written words struck a deep chord. He let go some more. Stage 3 was complete.

Now that I was comfortably in charge, I realized that perhaps my dad might never fully leave the scene. To help him, I chose to involve him in areas in which his expertise clearly exceeded mine. In his case, he stood out as the industry leader regarding the technical aspects of the printing process. As my special consigliere for all things technical, he retained a productive but external role in our business. He happily accepted this new position. Stage 4 was complete. The baton had been passed—finally. Amen!

Insider Tip #35
You may find it impossible to envision a life away from the challenges and excitement of the business you've built. Losing such a large part of your world can be frightening. But don't let this impede the leadership-transfer process.

Not a Death Sentence

Some departing leaders—like my father—hate the word "retirement." Likening it to blasphemy, they say, "If I retire, I'll die!" But retirement—when the old regime moves aside to make way for the new one—is, and always has been, part of the natural order of things.

Following his difficult transition away from the day-to-day management of Arkay, my dad did embrace retirement. Today, more than ten years after he stepped aside, he enjoys traveling with my mother and spending quality time with my two sons. We also meet monthly to discuss, with great calm, the key issues of our business. He still provides invaluable feedback and asks the same relevant questions: "How's cash?" "How's this month's billing?" and "What's the maintenance plan for equipment?" He sleeps well now. I guess he really has transitioned completely. With tears in his eyes, he regularly says to me, "I'm so proud of you. It makes me so happy. Grandfather Max would be so proud of you too!"

For many, retiring encompasses more than traveling, golfing, or playing tennis. It presents an opportunity to continue contributing to society by applying the same leadership skills honed over a lifetime to the future. Succession planning offers the ideal time for you as CEO to start thinking about what's next. By taking inventory of your work and personal life, you can identify those things you have always wanted to accomplish but never had the time for—like volunteer work or teaching.

To do this, I recommend retreating to a quiet place where  you're not likely to be disturbed. Try to visualize a typical day or week in your future, after you have successfully passed the baton to your successor. Focus on the big picture—the free time you will have to pursue rewarding activities (whatever they may be) that can fill your life with renewed excitement. Be certain to write down your thoughts and feelings. By fully engaging in the succession-planning process, you can start exploring those new ideas now to see what resonates with you and what doesn't. This will help make the next step—the baton handoff—less traumatic.

Consider these suggestions:

Over the years, I have met a number of members in the Young Presidents' Organization who had to relinquish control of their companies because they were bought up by larger ones. Many of these peers were in their midforties, far too young to stop working. So they went on to found new businesses. Nothing is stopping you, as an older, retired leader, from doing the same, if that's your dream.

Or you could slip into a consultant or ambassadorship role on behalf of the family business, talking up the new CEO and management team to employees, customers, vendors, and stockholders. In such a position, you might obtain information helpful to your company that some of those people would feel uncomfortable sharing with the current leadership. You could harness this role by offering your services as an active board member to one or more companies in noncompeting fields.

I have also met incumbent CEOs who didn't feel at all as though their life would end once they stepped down. They're rare, I admit, but they do exist. For them, the opportunity to rediscover their families and make up for all they had missed during their leadership years made their retirement glass half-full, rather than half-empty.

> Over the years, I have met a number of members in the Young Presidents' Organization who had to relinquish control of their companies because they were bought up by larger ones.

Gerald Levin, former CEO of Time Warner, said this about his involuntary retirement: "In the beginning it is difficult because there's a loud silence and everything seems to change. All the touch points of your identity have dissolved. That's the initial feeling. But then there's the exhilaration that comes from establishing your true identity and finding your real purpose."

An Ongoing Process

Unlike my grandfather and my dad, I'm planning for my retirement—today. I'm following the succession-planning process and objectives laid out in this book as I prepare for entering the next chapter in my own work life.

For various reasons (among them that I *love* the people I work with and would miss them terribly), I am not looking forward to the time when I will be stepping down as CEO of Arkay. But I know it will come. We are all replaceable.

I'm the father of twin boys—either one or both may someday want to belong to the *fourth generation* of leadership at

Arkay. And so, for now, I will continue addressing all the legacy-planning, training, and leadership elements that will make for a smooth transition when that day arrives.

Passing the baton can be a highly educational and satisfying time for all involved—management, family, employees, customers, and vendors. Of course, as either the outgoing leader or the successor, you may periodically think the changeover will never happen. Like me, you may even feel as though you're taking two steps backward for every one forward.

But if you persevere with the process I've presented here and stay patient, you will be rewarded, ultimately achieving a successful segue into the next chapter of the company's life. Yes, a succession can occur without an unproductive emotional tug of war. For sure, it can appear almost seamless—a major event transpiring so quietly that no one notices.

As a result, your entire community will have confidence in the transition. With leadership in place and family roles understood, your business will continue to play an integral part in local life. Tax revenues and jobs will remain intact. Product quality will prevail. Customers at home and around the world will no longer anxiously wait to see if the new leader has the right stuff.

Everyone will likely agree that the immediate future looks bright. They'll see that although the apple didn't fall too far from the tree, it indeed tastes a bit different. But it will still be savored by all, today and in the future.

Insider Tip #36

Keep a journal of your evolution as CEO. This rich resource will guide generations to come as they enter the family business and then step aside for their successor.

You are not here merely to make a living. You are here in order to enable the world to live more amply, with greater vision, with finer spirit of hope and achievement. You are here to enrich the world and impoverish yourself if you forget the errand.

—**Woodrow Wilson**

Be sure to pay attention and learn everything
you can. I learned a great deal from my father.

—**Donald Trump**

The Kaneff Legacy
Three Generations in Photos

MAX KANEFF

1

2

5

3

4

Ar-Kay
printing co., inc.

200 HUDSON STREET • NEW YORK 13, N. Y.

6

Opposite: (1) Max Kaneff, pressman, Montreal Printing Company, 1919; (2) Max and Jenny Kaneff's wedding day, 1924; (3) Max views Arkay's first offset/lithography two-color press, 1953; (4) Bobst Die Cutting machine is moved into 200 Hudson Street, 1966; (5) Max bartends at 200 Hudson Street employee holiday party, 1957; (6) Ar-Kay logo, 1949. *Above*: (7) Max (center) and Rusty Rudoff (second from right) with pressmen at the one-color Kelly press, 1949.

1

2

3

HOWARD KANEFF

4

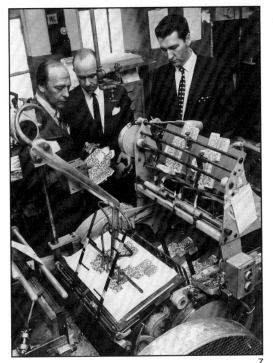

Opposite: (1) Howard, captain, Rochester Institute of Technology Fencing Team, 1949; (2) Howard at his desk, 200 Hudson Street, 1965; (3) Howard at Flushing Airport, Queens, New York, 1950; (4) Howard conducts an opening-day tour of the Hauppauge plant, 1969. *Above*: (5) 22 Arkay Drive: Arkay headquarters for forty years; (6) Heidelberg six-color offset printing press, 1990; (7) Howard inspects Kluge hot foil stamping press at 200 Hudson Street with Avon senior art director, Seymour Kent; (8) Howard and Cherry Kaneff at March of Dimes dinner honoring Howard with its Humanitarian of the Year Award, 1985.

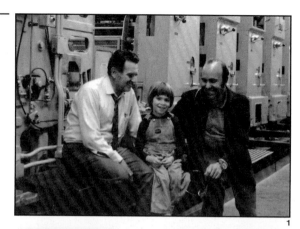

1

2

3

MITCHELL KANEFF

4

Opposite: (1) Rusty Rudoff, Mitchell (aged six), and Howard at the installation of a new five-color Miele offset printing press in Hauppauge, 1972; (2) Mitchell and Howard in Hauppauge, 1989; (3) Mitchell and Amy Kaneff, 2008; (4) Mitchell fronts his guitar collection, enjoying a riff on his five-string fretless bass. *Above*: (5) Mitchell and Howard celebrate Roanoke, Virginia, groundbreaking, 1995; (6) 62,000-square-food expansion of the Roanoke plant, 2008; (7) Mitchell and Howard attend Lifetime Achievement Award Celebration (Arkay 85th anniversary), 2007; (8) Cherry, Leonard Lauder, Mitchell, Howard, and Amy at Arkay's 80th anniversary celebration, 2002; (9) Mitchell with sons Josh and Max atop a seven-color double flexo coater Man Roland printing press, Roanoke ribbon-cutting ceremony, 2008.

APPENDIXES

Tell me and I'll forget; show me and I may remember; involve me and I'll understand.

—Chinese Proverb

Insider Tips at a Glance

1 Decide if the family business really excites you. Feeling passionate about taking over the organization and genuinely wanting to shape its future are key not only to achieving a smooth transition but also to making a positive, lasting impact.

2 Get clear about your goals to quickly gain the respect of the entire organization for addressing the company's future. Most important, you'll feel good about yourself for starting to move toward that future by developing a vision of it.

3 Examine family values and emotional issues as they relate to the business *before* you take over. Trying to do this later, when you're on the job, is like trying to get the lay of the land from a foxhole.

4 Don't hesitate to turn to consultants for help. Not only can they shave years off the transition process, but by reducing stress, they can *add* years to your life as well.

5 Hit the ground running by reviewing your relatives' salaries prior to taking the helm. Establish fair compensation for each position based on performance and market standards, not on a family member's demands.

6 Be honest with yourself. If you don't share your predecessor's passion, do him, yourself, and everyone else a favor and relinquish the role to another successor or buyer. Go all the way—or go home.

7 How you enter the business and how you leave it are connected. The degree to which you understand and honor this connection will determine how successful you are as a CEO.

8 Shooting all the messengers won't change the facts. To create a healthy working environment and position your company for success, you must welcome all the news—the good and the bad—and review data objectively.

9 Family businesses often get mired down in the status quo— but to stay vibrant, companies must constantly evolve. When you assume leadership, trust your intuition to point you in new directions.

10 Remember that projecting your good intentions on rivals can yield unsavory results: a friend today could easily turn into a competitor tomorrow.

11 To revitalize and grow your company, eliminate generations-old informal and erratic practices. Discipline plus empowerment plus accountability equals progress.

12 Make transparency an integral part of your business culture. It is essential to achieving financial consistency.

13 You will undoubtedly feel overwhelmed with the tasks of your new position, so take time before assuming control to fully evaluate the skills and values of working family members and the other personnel awaiting you.

14 Your company's health will dictate whether you need to keep anyone from the previous team or start from scratch. Don't rush the decision process—but don't take too long either—and stay open to changing course if you realize you've made a wrong decision.

15 If a weak link exists within your core leadership team, you must remove the individual—or the integrity, resolve, and strength of the entire team will be irrevocably compromised.

16 With all the stresses of transitioning into a family business, you could easily hang on to outside advisors too long. Cut them loose—even though you feel like you're free-falling. If they helped you once, you can always hire them again.

17 During meetings with industrial psychologists, establish an agenda and follow-up actions to maintain momentum. A succession, like a living organism, must be nurtured—or stagnation will set in.

18 Recruit and interview all potential advisors carefully. The decisions you make jointly will significantly affect your family's future.

19 You may love your work, but you must get away from it occasionally to return fresher and recharged, especially when you run a family business. How you spend your downtime doesn't matter—as long as you give yourself this gift.

20 Struggling to fit work, family, health, and personal activities into your schedule can forever be used as an excuse for not being able to find the time. Don't surrender to procrastination—jump right in!

21 Begin succession planning a minimum of five to ten years prior to the new leader's taking control. This will provide sufficient time for reviewing and fixing your plan—and some fixing will almost always be needed.

22 To increase the likelihood of a positive transition, the CEO, successor, and family stakeholders must fully dedicate themselves to the process and participate in all decision making.

23 An effective succession may involve selling the business or choosing dual leaders—explore all possibilities and be willing to brainstorm creative solutions.

24 Don't kid yourself into thinking that the leadership transfer in a family business will magically work itself out because blood is thicker than water. You must take deliberate, impartial action to locate the best new leader.

25 Look for passion as the top quality in your replacement. Your company's future depends on having a leader who can excite and motivate people.

26 To set the stage for future success, the current leadership must give a successor-in-training the freedom to make mistakes. So often, CEOs stall the transition process because they're afraid to see their replacement fail.

27 Upon succession, set a plan to deliver immediate and measurable results to one area of the business. A quick success will build confidence in the new leader, the new team—and the organization.

28 Take advantage of recessions and other low-income periods to transfer more value to the heir apparent and reduce tax consequences.

29 At the start of the transition, the outgoing and incoming leaders must work together as internists in evaluating the company's financial health.

30 Use external auditors to objectively review your company's financials since they can recognize potential problems and present workable solutions to improve your bottom line.

31 An estate-planning dream team can ensure that all pertinent documents are properly drafted, accurately signed, and safely stored in an accessible place ready for delivery at the right time.

32 Spend the time and money to draw up estate-planning documents and keep them safe. It's a small price to pay for the security of knowing that no one will be able to claim more from your estate than you have entitled them to.

33 As the owner-leader of a family business, you should follow a well-planned, long-term gifting strategy that gives everything to your heirs during your lifetime—so that you ultimately die with nothing.

34 Letting go is a critical part of a successful transition. In fact, from the moment you take over a business, you must begin emotionally preparing for the day you relinquish power—otherwise, chaos will likely ensue.

35 You may find it impossible to envision a life away from the challenges and excitement of the business you've built. Losing such a large part of your world can be frightening. But don't let this impede the leadership-transfer process.

36 Keep a journal of your evolution as CEO. This rich resource will guide generations to come as they enter the family business and then step aside for their successor.

Consultant Resources

- **Family Legacy** (www.efamilylegacy.com or 1-800-526-2846) offers a range of nationally available services for family-held businesses, including family communication; owning versus managing; strategic planning and management planning; clarifying career development goals of family members; marketing analysis; and the valuation, buying, and selling of businesses.

- **SPARDATA** (www.spardata.com or 1-800-895-4100) functions as a professional appraiser whose primary field of expertise is the valuation of privately owned businesses. While the IRS does not positively view the use of personal accountants in this area, SPARDATA—as a third party and independent voice—is the perfect antidote. These consultants are also an excellent resource for advice on gifting, as well as on transferring property.

- **Dr. Joel Goldberg** (www.careerconsultants-us.com or 1-800-723-1306) is president and founder of Career Consultants, a full-service human resources consulting firm specializing in helping corporations and sports teams improve their human resources and resolve organizational issues. Advisors tailor their comprehensive, integrated, and practical services to their clients' needs.

- **Dr. Jerry Larson & Associates, Inc.** (www.drjlarson.com or 1-401-374-7183) provides services in executive and organizational coaching, leadership development and team building, emotional intelligence development, and change and transition management.

- **Family Business Magazine** (www.familybusinessmagazine .com or 1-800-637-4464) offers a wealth of information on small business management, transition issues, and many other related subjects, as well as links to other useful sites, such as www.fambizadvice.com.

- **The Family Business Institute (FBI)** (www.familybusiness institute.com or 1-877-326-2493) provides "emergency room medicine" to help nurse family-owned businesses back to health and create a foundation for a prosperous future. Services include roundtable conferences, speakers, newsletters, and many other useful tools and resources.

ABOUT THE AUTHOR

Mitchell Kaneff is the chairman and CEO of Arkay Packaging, an eighty-eight-year-old family-owned and family-operated leader in the folding-carton industry. Under Mitchell's direction, Arkay provides innovative product-packaging solutions to companies such as Estée Lauder, Procter & Gamble, Elizabeth Arden, and L'Oréal.

Founded by Mitchell's grandfather, Max Kaneff, in 1922, this third-generation family business began on the Lower East Side of New York City. After Mitchell's father, Howard, took the helm, Arkay continued to grow and dominate the market by adapting new technologies.

Working in the family business since high school, Mitchell received his B.S. in printing management and sciences from the Rochester Institute of Technology. He has led Arkay and its 185 employees since 1997, consistently defining and redefining its vision and goals.

Mitchell's appreciation for customer satisfaction and his understanding of the industry have solidified partnerships with key customers, earning his company Supplier of the Year Award several years running. Additionally, with its focus on green strategies, Arkay recently received the Agfa GreenWorks™ Environmental Recognition Award and is proud to be affiliated with—and certified by—Sustainable Forestry Initiative, Community Energy, and Forest Stewardship Council.

Mitchell passionately follows both professional and personal pursuits. In addition to being a member of the Young Presidents' Organization, he enjoys membership in the Hauppauge Industrial Association, Printing Industries of America, Cosmetic Industry Buyers and Suppliers, Graphic Arts Technical Foundation, and the Graphic Source LLC. Mitchell is also a dedicated supporter of community activities as well as a proud donor to the Taubman Museum of Art in Roanoke, Virginia.

Among Mitchell's many personal interests is his deep love of music. In 1997, he released *Renaissance Man*, a CD collection of his original music for which he designed and patented the packaging and provided the art and photography. In his continuous quest for creative mastery, Mitchell is presently studying jazz guitar—his CD of jazz standards will be available soon—and playing with The Young Presidents (www.theyoungpresidents.com), a rock band performing in the New York metropolitan area.

Mitchell lives in New York City with his wife, Amy, and his twin sons, Max and Josh.

For more about Mitchell's life and work, visit his website: www.mitchellkaneff.com.